Deepwater Ports
in the United States

Tobey L. Winters

The Praeger Special Studies program—utilizing the most modern and efficient book production techniques and a selective worldwide distribution network—makes available to the academic, government, and business communities significant, timely research in U.S. and international economic, social, and political development.

Deepwater Ports
in the United States

An Economic and
Environmental
Impact Study

PRAEGER SPECIAL STUDIES IN U.S. ECONOMIC, SOCIAL, AND POLITICAL ISSUES

Praeger Publishers   New York   London

Library of Congress Cataloging in Publication Data

Winters, Tobey L   1944-
    Deepwater ports in the United States.

    (Praeger special studies in U.S. economic, social,
and political issues)
    Bibliography: p. 179
    Includes index.
    1. Harbors—Environmental aspects—United States.
2. Harbors—United States.   I. Title.
HE553.W55   387.1'0973   76-12885
ISBN 0-275-23250-6

PRAEGER PUBLISHERS

200 Park Avenue, New York, N.Y. 10017, U.S.A.

Published in the United States of America in 1977
by Praeger Publishers, Inc.

ACKNOWLEDGMENTS

I thank Guthrie Birkhead and Jesse Burkhead of the Maxwell School of Syracuse University. Their timely assistance and comments on early drafts were instrumental in improving on the whole. John Henning was patient with attempts to make the econometric treatment fit the subject.

On the subject of transportation economics, David R. Miller was particularly helpful and informative on a range of issues. J. David Jordan and I have worked on a variety of transportation planning problems together. His approach to planning helped to clarify modeling in air quality and transportation.

Betty Ringer has typed much more than I anticipated. Her help and way of lending it are appreciated.

Robert Rothenhausler was encouraging and a helping friend throughout the ordeal of research and writing. His company was always welcomed.

Leslie and Fara improvised on many a dull weekend, if not without complaint, at least without rancor. Both Leslie and Bob were supportive when it was needed.

CONTENTS

LIST OF TABLES, FIGURES, AND MAP

CONVERSION TABLE

	Factor Used
Barrels in a long ton	7.5
American gallons in a barrel	42.0
Barrels in a cubic meter	.159
Cubic meters to barrels	6.29
Btus in a barrel	5,800,000
Barrels per day to tons per year	50.00
Refining/throughput per day/per annum	365-day year

Deepwater Ports
in the United States

Since the first commercial discoveries of petroleum in Pennsylvania, oil men have struggled with the problem of how to move crude oil to market. Deepwater ports represent one more step in the competitive struggle with rivals, with the cost of transportation, and with innovation. New terminals, supertankers, and pipelines are an engineering challenge. From such facilities other futures may be possible--the development of towns and the founding of large enterprises.

Viewed in the contexts of cost, innovation, and improving a company's market share or increasing profits, deepwater ports represent an opportunity. In the past, oil companies have sought such opportunities and have joined interests on large enterprises.

Petroleum has always been an aggressive and innovative business. Even when John D. Rockefeller, through Standard Oil, controlled 90 to 95 percent of the refinery capacity and 92 percent of crude oil supplies, there was intense rivalry. And, despite this power, his competition succeeded in reducing Standard Oil's hegemony in the market. Before Standard Oil was broken up by antitrust legislation prior to World War I, it had lost ground. By 1911 Standard Oil controlled 64 percent of the refinery capacity and controlled very little of the soon to be important Gulf Coast crude oil supplies.

The recent past has provided an example of control and competition. During the 1973-74 energy crisis, many service stations and a few independent oil distributors were forced out of business. The market processes worked, but to the detriment of the independent operator. With no integrated oil company affiliation the independents could not obtain priority in fuel distribution.

Deepwater ports represent an opportunity to cut costs and successfully compete. As a common carrier there would be protection from discrimination in access to terminal facilities, but with the oil industry locational advantage is a familiar route to a greater share of the market through lower transportation costs. In the early years, John D. Rockefeller simply secured more favorable railroad freight rates than his rivals. Today deepwater ports offer market control through the real economic benefits of a low-cost and high-volume delivery system.

Looking at oil company history, the first oil was taken out on horse-drawn wagons by a group of hard-bargaining teamsters. From wagon and road, the next leg of the journey to market would have been the railroad or barge. If the railroad had no waterborne competition, there may have been different competing rail lines. Even so, the introduction of the pipeline became an effective alternative to the teamster and the railroad. Today, the deepwater terminal is an attractive alternative to existing ports. And viewed by the industry, this alternative is both logical and expected. Innovation has not been shunned, and despite the concentration of the market in the petroleum industry, operating cost and productivity have not been a problem.

Aside from the lessons and history of the industry, there are other ways to view deepwater ports. From the point of view of a proponent or opponent to port development, the tradition and perspective of the industry is an important consideration. Another perspective with its own internal logic is the evaluation of the transportation planner.

Measured by relative cost, accessibility, or other indexes of relative effort, producing and consuming regions can be brought closer together. The Gulf or East Coast of the United States may become more accessible to Kuwait or Iran. This improvement in accessibility is not measured by trip time, but on the basis of barrels of oil delivered per unit of cost. Existing ports are deficient because these ports cannot accommodate vessels with drafts from 65 to 80 feet.

Because deepwater ports are used in much of the world where oil is produced or imported for consumption, existing long-haul waterborne oil to the United States must either be shipped in tankers of about 50,000 deadweight tons (rather than 150,000 to 300,000 dwt), or the oil must be transferred from large carriers to smaller vessels at some transshipment facility in Canada or the Bahamas. The ratio of the quantity of oil delivered daily has been calculated to be on the order of 4:1 or 2:1 for large tankers using deepwater ports compared to maximum permissible size vessels using existing facilities.

More than 6 million barrels daily were imported to the United States during 1974. Of this amount more than 1 million barrels

came from Canada and Venezuela in the form of crude oil, while
slightly less than 1 million barrels arrived as products. The remaining 4 million barrels of both crude and refined oil were available from more distant ports, principally the Middle East and
Africa.[1] Four million barrels represent about 23 percent of the
U.S. petroleum market. This is a sizable market with a potentially
cheaper source of transportation.

Clearly such a market, particularly if it is expanding, provides considerable cost savings. Not only can more oil be delivered
with fewer ships, but cost is cheaper per barrel delivered. Consequently, the more oil delivered per trip, the greater the savings.
Scheduling of vessels, and the proper mix of fleet between small and
large vessels, are factors, but the incentive to deliver greater volumes of oil in larger vessels is both an economic inducement and an
engineering challenge. Moreover, the limit on savings due to vessel size has not been determined.

There is, of course, a certain magnificence about huge tankers entering a twenty-first century port. Most other engineering
works are much less impressive in scale and scope. The dollar
savings from such an investment will be calculated, but these savings do not tell the whole story. Deepwater ports and vessels are a
technological innovation. Ports may bring changes to the petroleum
industry beyond lower transport cost. One possibility is that deepwater ports will lead to development.

Development is not always of much concern to transportation
planners. The ecologist or economist asks the question of whether
development can be expected from deepwater port facilities. The
question is germane to whether environment degradation would be
expected, or whether increased community employment and terminal-
related economic activities might follow as a result of a deepwater
port. Whether a refinery or a petrocomplex is either a desirable or
inevitable result of a deepwater port, is one of the questions that
should be amenable to analysis and evaluation. Certain economic
and environmental factors shall be addressed herein.

This book focuses on some of the traditional economic and
planning evaluation techniques to view deepwater ports in the larger
context of the competition among organized interests in U.S. society.
It is considered insufficient that benefit/cost-like comparisons are
made. Rather, evaluation techniques will be used in conjunction
with the point of view and interests of the groups who support or
oppose deepwater facilities.

Throughout the book, the perspectives of the petroleum industry, the environmentalist, and the transportation planner will be
presented in a technical framework. One such framework is demand
analysis; of concern is how demand analysis can indicate the need

and opportunity for deepwater ports. Another framework is benefit/
cost analysis, as presented in terms of how ecological alternatives
are compared to the economic benefits.

One of the persistent questions this book addresses is the extent to which deepwater ports foster development. Some traditional
economic techniques are used to understand how terminal decisions
relate to probable development outcomes.

Important to the context of how deepwater terminals are examined is the relationship of such facilities to an overall energy
future for the United States. To set this policy context, the nation's
energy future is explored as it pertains to the import of foreign oil.

Deepwater ports are explored in a setting of an uncertain
energy future with competing groups seeking their separate objectives. The background for the evaluation is an industry that seeks
ports, and local groups that oppose such ports for reasons of ecology
and community preference. At the state level there are elements of
both a development viewpoint and a conservation policy. Although
all views are expressed at all levels, the potential adverse impacts
are more apt to fall on regions and localities. Uncertainty is addressed through an exploration of alternatives.

OBSERVATIONS ON DEVELOPMENT

Transportation projects have had an important place in the development of regions. Development has been the aim of nations and
cities, particularly in the twentieth century. A transportation project of sufficient scope will be of regional and even national importance. There is some doubt whether it is always possible to equate
transportation projects with development, or to assume that the size
of the engineering undertaking is an adequate index of development
consequences. Nevertheless, a transportation project such as a
deepwater port must be considered as capable of fostering future development. The question posed here is whether a deepwater port is
a sufficient cause for a sequence of developmental steps.

Development has been studied primarily by economists and
historians. Both have contributed to the question of how cities and
regions grow. Whereas the historian has been primarily descriptive,
perhaps in an analytical framework (such as Eric Lampard), the
economist has chosen to provide theories on growth. It would be
interesting to specify how theorists from Von Thunen to Walter Isard
or Melvin Greenhut have contributed to our understanding of urban
economics.[2] In terms of the impact of deepwater ports on development, such a review may be misleading, for the port-siting decision
may be more dependent upon what government allows than on what

locational factors would logically dictate. Although it is common to use concepts such as multiplier effects and induced growth, a single project may not have significant effects on regional change.

In a mixed economy without strong regional planning, a deep-water port represents project planning. Project planning may not represent a real commitment to eventual development of a petro-complex and subsequently a new community. In France, where regional planning with national government support leads to development of new ports such as La Fos near Marseilles, it may be expected that the theories of economic growth of communities are a reasonable guide to the future.[3] In the United States, however, this kind of regional land-use planning is absent. In a federal system of government with a much stronger private sector than in Europe, regional planning is not a guide to the future. Accordingly, development must be evaluated in terms of whether conditions are such that the project itself is likely to spur further development.

In the United States, evaluating the effect of a project rather than a regional plan is not to say that the plan itself does not contain useful inferences about community objectives. Rather, the plan does not represent a real commitment by any organized force in society. Behind every project, however, such a force can be discerned. As the starting point for evaluation of development, the project is the focus of concern. The growth dynamics of communities must be understood, but community growth is not immune to government intervention and control.

Impact analysis is one means by which projects are evaluated for growth consequences. In a political environment, however, these narrow calculations of impacts are usually ignored. The social purpose ascribed to large engineering projects is usually presented in symbolic and tangible ways that indicate a benign future-- a future that is only obtainable with public acceptance of a project. This means presentation, much in the style of Robert Moses, is meant to sway public policy. Since public support is needed to generate approval of a project, the claims of far-reaching consequences are in the U.S. tradition. On the other hand, these consequences now intrude upon environmental-impact evaluation, which reaches just the opposite conclusion about the merits of the project.

As a result of this political process, it has become difficult to determine how policy and planning could shape the future. Almost any important land-use decision becomes an individual battle wholly unrelated (in the political process) to past decisions and most certainly unrelated to future decisions. This competitive environment of how people feel about the area in which they work and live may be the overwhelming factor in whether a specific project is viewed as leading to economic growth or environmental decline. These concerns are somewhat independent of what impact analysis shows. In a less polarized situation, there may be planning devices that can be used which would ensure that neither polar result occurs.

The project as a battleground has been the chief obstacle to planning. As the development aspects of deepwater ports are explored, it is done with recognition that the dynamics of deepwater port decisions may be quite independent or contrary to a reasonable presentation of alternatives. For this reason deepwater ports are viewed somewhat more in the context of game theory than as scholarly cost/benefit and environmental-impact evaluation. The problem is not only to use evaluation techniques to explore alternative outcomes, but to indicate what circumstances are likely to lead to which outcomes.

Every transportation decision must address the question of what can be expected, as well as the question of what alternatives are foreseen. It is the political process that puts the project in the center of the arena and is responsible for this game-theory perspective. A less roundabout way of saying the same thing is to note that political and economic decisions need some common ground for evaluation. This common ground need not be reduced or elevated to the language of mathematics, but it should be amenable to logical analysis.

A NOTE ON TECHNOLOGY

One of the ingredients in growth and development that is difficult to evaluate is technology. New technology titillates the imagination. Allied with a perceivable social purpose, new technology has formed a part of futuristic visions of society. In fact, most futurists are exceedingly more adept in describing the alternatives in the technological world than in the social world. Technology and economic development are often the forces which combine to persuade the otherwise unmoved that transportation improvements are necessary. An older theory of social change states that it is, in fact, technology that sets off growth and it is culture that lags behind, accommodating itself to technological innovation.[4] Even the skeptical and the opposed often believe in the inevitability of technology. Some will argue temporary containment or modification of technological change, either to limit or soften the impact of change.

The specifics of a project, however, rarely encapsulate much technological change. Such change is a result of a long delay and a series of adjustments. The specific project may mark a turning point, but it may just as well be a development failure or have a minimal impact on growth. Often a new technology is tried somewhere

and does not diffuse more widely. For example, large crude carriers may merely reinforce existing locations of refining and chemical activity without a wider economic impact.

   Environmental considerations may not be all negative. Perhaps
better routine tanker operations can substantially reduce most oil
spills. Accidents may be avoided more easily through carefully built,
very large carriers. If it were true that deepwater ports were an
ecological advantage, the opportunity to combine profit and cleaner
seas should not be missed. Equally important are the landside effects of a new refinery and whether "new source" performance for
air and water quality are such as to promote a cleaner environment.
These impacts should be looked at for what they promise and for the
likely reality.

   As there is magnificence in the large carrier and twenty-first
century ports, there is a good deal of childishness in engineering
size for its own sake. Is a larger ship just a larger ship built for
profit and resold like a used car, greatly depreciated and unsafe?
By what sleight of hand does size, or its opposite, miniaturization,
do much for man? Often it is enough to say that something can be
done, and therefore it should be done.

   Traditionally, the U.S. government has supported technical
innovation in transportation. The competitive position of the United
States has often been used as the compelling reason to innovate, ad-
vance new technology, or simply to take leadership. Higher costs
have often been ignored in the face of foreign nations taking the lead,
dominating U.S. industry, or as a result of a future (if ill-defined)
threat to security. The oil industry, maritime interests, and defense
industries have obtained privileged positions based upon their provi-
sion of certain essential commodities. Despite the murkiness of such
determination of national interest, it continues to occur in the minds
of policymakers. Skepticism and caution are needed in defining what
is imperative as a national "transportation policy," a national "energy
policy," or a national "land-use" policy. Among the considerations
in formulating policy should be consequences of a particular course
of action and the balance between a general national objective and
the local impact of pursuing that objective. As policy is a matter of
choice, some framework must be provided. Demand analysis, impact analysis, and some approximation of a benefit/cost balance
sheet are all devices through which policies can be examined.

FACILITY PLANNING AND DEMAND ANALYSIS

   It is customary to begin the discussion of transportation facility planning with the analysis of demand. The reasons for the focus

on demand analysis are various. First, demand is usually an accepted rationale for shifting away from the existing arrangement.
The usual view is that demand is an exogenous variable in the transport system. The transport system, whether a road network, pipeline network, or public transit system, has some limiting capacity
to satisfy transport needs at a given level of service. The system
itself can be described in terms of level of service--usually defined
as the ability to deliver a commodity through the transport system
in a given period of time. When the demand, which arises from
forces external to the transport system, puts a load on the system
exceeding the desired level of service, the usual interpretation is
that the system should be expanded. Other reasons can be put forward for improving and expanding transportation systems, but
demand is a most powerful reason.

External demand provides an opportunity to charge the beneficiaries directly for any transport system improvements. If level
of service can be adequately defined, then the users of the system
can perceive improvements. Often the users are or should be willing to pay for the new services that are provided. If the charges to
the users are adequate to pay for the investment in system expansion, then the improvements are self-liquidating. There is a com-
monsense appeal to allowing the users to pay for system expansion
and letting this mechanism be the rationale for expanding the transport system.

As an external force, demand can then provide an objective
measure of whether transport systems with their externalities have
a legitimate claim to expansion. At minimum, a broadly defined
group, called users, can be identified as being the beneficiaries of
the investment. This group has some broader claims to public
policy than landowners, contractors, or businessmen. The assumption that a group called "users" must be identified at all is based
upon the possible costs the investment may create for the public at
large--either because the project requires public funds or special
advantages or because externalities imposed on nonusers are considerable.

This foregoing description is simple, but there are some real
transport problems in defining the appropriate level of service.
Obvious, too, are the nonusers who benefit from new system investment. Moreover, a transport system may be subject to unusual
circumstances, such as peaking or periodic reduction in system
capacity, which require attention in facility planning. Peaking may
in fact be a regular phenomenon and be an integral part of the difficulty of charging each user for the cost that the user imposes on
system operation or expansion. Nevertheless, increasing demand
is the environment in which transport systems are expanded.

Moreover, this simple explanation alone includes several assumptions that are subject to analysis in transport-system planning.

The first assumption in the statement that demand is the explanation for facility expansion is rejection of the notion that the system expansion itself will either shift demand or induce demand. This particular point is central to all latter-day transport system modeling of urban travel.

Without discussing the literature, it can be said that there are two distinct views about demand. The first view considers demand to be the demand for the use of the system, through level of service related to the capacity of the system to accommodate that demand.[5] Accordingly, the interaction of the demand and capacity of the system defines the level of service, and in order to attain a higher level of service new capacity must be provided. In this view, there is no relationship between the new capacity and any future demand, that is, all planning starts with demand.

Usually this view, which will be called the engineering view, for lack of a better term, is one for assessing the need for capital expenditure. Demand is considered a function of independent variables, for example, income, growth, or trade expansion.

It is often possible to provide a higher level of service through better scheduling, management, or proper queuing. An example may be the investigation of flight operations improvements over the years that have increased the number of airplanes that can safely use an airport in a given period of time. Numerous examples can be given and such improvements have been addressed in operations research. Generally it is assumed, although often wrongly, that such techniques have been fully examined.

It should be noted that the engineering view is a description of how system expansion has been advanced in public policy analysis. It is assumed that the profitability aspects are taken care of either through financial analysis or, if a public project, through benefit/cost analysis. Given that some improvement is required, the transportation planner must be capable of analyzing his transport network to identify the most useful improvements to the system.

The second view of demand does not consider that demand is independent but begins with the notion that the demand for the transport system is a function of the level of service it provides, the price charged for that service, or some combination of level of service variables and price variables. This view rejects the notion of capacity and defines demand as capable of total increases or market shifts depending upon the kind of service provided and the prices charged to the users. Supply is then accommodated to demand through price (and subsidy) as users indicate their preferences. This economic, as opposed to engineering, view is the approach where supply and demand can be simultaneously determined. New supply at a price creates its own demand. Again, the financial considerations are assumed to have been taken care of through profitability and market analysis or by benefit/cost analysis.

One of the weaknesses of this second view is that demand may not exist in sufficient quantity or a demand shift may be acquired at a cost that exceeds the benefits of moving to some higher level of satisfaction. The engineering view is usually advanced as a rationale for increasing a specific service for which the level of use can be identified. The second economic view is normally advanced when yet unproven but marketable investment is advocated. Generally, the situation is clouded by different externalities attached to the investment decision. Moreover, the decision is confused by the availability of public funds for front-end investment, for payment of any deficits, or for financial security to investors.

The distinction between users and nonusers is essential in the discussion of externalities. Except for a few windfall gains, on the whole the users of the system are beneficiaries and the nonusers bear the burden of external costs. There may be important exceptions, for certainly there are both subclasses of users and subclasses of nonusers and these subclasses are not alike. The nonusers may be strongly for, strongly against, or completely indifferent to transportation system improvements. Nevertheless, the rationale for investment is provided through the vehicle of increased demand for the transport system and the level of service it provides.

Two issues should be mentioned about demand for deepwater ports. The first is the effect of deepwater ports on the price of foreign oil. Lower-cost oil for the petroleum refiner is a benefit that may or may not be passed on to the consumer. The second issue is the impact of the demand shift as deepwater ports replace existing oil transport systems. These two issues require consideration along with the environmental and land-use impact of deepwater ports.

On the one hand, the engineering view of deepwater investment would examine the prospect of increased oil imports and determine when capacity (or low cost) considerations require facility expansion. The second economic view would examine transport pricing with deepwater ports and estimate to what extent deepwater facilities attract users. The first view is the traditional approach of transportation planners while the latter is more familiar to businessmen. In each approach need is differently defined and in each approach there would be a different outlook on externalities. Whenever the benefits and costs of deepwater ports are discussed, the demand for investment centers on one or both of these perspectives.

SEADOCK AND LOOP

Two projects on the Gulf Coast are likely to be approved and built. Both of these deepwater ports are designed to handle a significant portion of the crude oil to be imported to the United States. Both projects are offshore terminals using monobuoy systems in deep water for tanker docking. The LOOP Project has decided to use a single anchor leg monobuoy (SALM), while SEADOCK will use that system or the catenary anchor leg monobuoy (CALM). Both projects will eventually have six monobuoys, if demand warrants expansion. For the SEADOCK project crude oil will be pumped through underwater pipelines to a tank farm and with LOOP pipelines will deliver oil to salt domes.*

SEADOCK will be built about 25 miles south of Freeport, Texas, serving the many refineries along the Texas coast from Corpus Christi to Lake Charles, Louisiana. In 1975 this market area for SEADOCK contained 3,318 thousand barrels of refining capacity. Given this concentration it is reasonable that SEADOCK is designed for a throughput of 2.5 to 4 million barrels of crude oil. For the most part this crude oil will be shipped from the Middle East.

The LOOP project will serve refineries in the New Orleans area and east to Alabama. The project will be 18 miles south of Louisiana with onshore facilities in La Fourche Parish. The buoy, pipeline, and storage system will be designed for 3.4 million barrels. Rather than serve extensive coastal refining, LOOP's projects depend upon the Capline pipeline serving the mid-West. The pipeline system will serve refineries in Louisiana through the St. James pipeline and extend northward to Michigan. There are now east-west connecting pipelines along Capline's north-south route. The 1975 estimated refinery capacity for refineries served by LOOP, St. James, and Capline pipelines is 3,288,400 barrels.

Both port projects will be located in water depths of 100 feet or more. The center of activity offshore will be the offshore platform rising 95 feet from the water. On this platform will be the permanent quarters and port-operations base for the port superintendent, mooring master, and other port-operations work force. The platform will contain oil cleanup facilities, mooring launches, a weather station, and an oil pumping station.

---

*These descriptions are based on SEADOCK and LOOP applications for licenses submitted to the U.S. Coast Guard, Washington, D.C., December 1975.

Arranged in a wide circle about the platform will be the six buoys, each about 8,000 feet from the platform. Initially SEADOCK will build four buoys and LOOP will build three. Each buoy will allow a very large crude carrier to dock and rotate in a 1,500-foot radius about the buoy on an anchor leg. Each buoy will be about 8,000 feet from an adjacent buoy to allow ample area for maneuvering and safety. Diagrammatically, the offshore system is a platform box with six underwater spindles. At the end of each spindle is a buoy. The spindles are underwater feeder pipelines connected to three main pipelines that reach shore. From a distance only the platform and the tankships will be visible. The tankships will dwarf the buoy around which they swing one and one-half miles from the platform or the nearest tankship.

When the tankship is docked near the buoy, mooring launches will bring anchor lines to the tanker. After securing the tanker to its buoy pivot, the launches will bring the oil hoses to the tankship. The pumping platform and pipeline system will be capable of unloading a 200,000 dwt vessel through the hoses and pipeline in about 15 hours.

The crude oil will then be pumped on shore through underwater pipelines; eventually there will be three pipelines, with diameters of 48 to 56 inches, at each port. From the pipelines the oil enters onshore storage tanks at the SEADOCK site near Freeport, Texas. In total the tanks will hold 22 million barrels; each tank will be from 48 feet to 68 feet high and about 400 feet in diameter. Unlike SEADOCK, the LOOP pipeline system carries oil much further upland, to the Clovelly Salt domes in Louisiana. Owing to the 25-mile trip to Clovelly, an intermediate pumping station will be needed near the halfway point from the buoy to the salt domes.

The SEADOCK project application is not explicit on how the oil will move from the tank farm on its 8,600 acres of land near Freeport. Barge and pipelines will probably be used, depending on each refiner's access to waterways. The LOOP project, however, will pump most of its oil through the St. James pipeline, serving southern Louisiana and from there northward via Capline.

Both projects would begin construction in 1977 if the applications were approved. So far LOOP shareholders have spent more than $6 million and SEADOCK owners have spent nearly $5 million. A good portion of these funds have been used to research and evaluate the environmental and safety considerations of the projects, as well as for design and preliminary engineering.

If approved early, both projects are designed for operation by 1980, when most of the construction would be completed. For the first construction phase, SEADOCK estimates that it will spend $659 million and LOOP expects to spend $348 million; for all construction

SEADOCK expects to spend $865 million and LOOP $738 million.
The shareholders, primarily the oil companies, are expected to be
the principal users of the system.

To what extent these two projects will shape future petroleum
investment in the United States depends upon a number of factors.
The first is the continuous availability of foreign crude oil and its
price. A second important factor is the extent and nature of expansion in domestic energy production. A third is whether the East
Coast will also allow deepwater development, such as in Maine, or
whether Canada and the Bahama Islands will serve the East Coast.
A fourth consideration is other developments likely to have impact
on refinery expansion, such as the price of crude oil, domestic or
foreign, and refinery expansion plans of foreign nations.

Each of these topics will be taken up in turn, focusing on deepwater port projects and their impacts. Although SEADOCK and
LOOP represent the most likely developments, the question of East
Coast port projects is also discussed in some detail. Deepwater
port development takes place in an uncertain world. Competition
exists among shareholders of the various projects, usually the large
petroleum companies; it involves regions of the country with disparate views on growth; and it concerns the competition between environmental and economic issues, perceptions, and impacts. Moreover, a great amount of uncertainty overlies public and private
interest, even when the best course of action of each separate group
is well known and strongly held.

NOTES

1. "Midyear Report," Oil and Gas Journal (July 29, 1974):
130. By 1975 overall imports had increased slightly, Canada had
reduced exports, and domestic refiners imported fewer products and
more crude oil.

2. Of particular interest are present writers who have con-
tributed to location theory rather than other closely related areas of
regional economics. A few key works would include: E. M. Hoover,
The Location of Economic Activity (New York: McGraw-Hill, 1948);
Walter Isard, Methods of Regional Analysis (Cambridge, Mass.:
M.I.T. Press, 1960); and Melvin Greenhut, Microeconomics and the
Space Economy (Chicago: Scott, Foresman, 1963). Appraisal of the
field past and present can be found in three works: Harry W.
Richardson, ed., Regional Economics: A Reader (New York: St.
Martins Press, 1970); L. Needleman, ed., Regional Analysis
(Baltimore: Penguin Books, 1968); and John Friedman and William
Alonso, eds., Regional Development and Planning (Cambridge, Mass.:
M.I.T. Press, 1964).

3. For example, Niles Hansen credits Perroux's theory of growth poles to present-day French development policy. See Hansen, "Development Pole Theory in a Regional Context, " in Richardson, Regional Economics, pp. 134-49.

4. This is basically William F. Ogburn's theory. See Otis Dudley Duncan, ed. , William F. Ogburn on Culture and Social Change (Chicago: University of Chicago Press, 1964). Joseph Schumpeter thought technological change important to innovation and as a force in business cycles in Joseph Alois Schumpeter, The Theory of Economic Development (Cambridge: Oxford University Press, 1961).

5. Traffic engineering is an example of this thinking. An application to people movement is embodied in highway design criteria in the Highway Research Board, Highway Capacity Manual (Washington, D.C., 1965). Most pure network problems embody this concept.

2

DEMAND AND
CONSUMPTION OF
PETROLEUM

If deepwater ports were built solely to meet foreign oil imports, and if such imports could be estimated with reasonable accuracy, then it would be possible to estimate the total needed port throughput capacity. Since this capacity (measured in barrels per day) would necessarily be spread out to serve various regions along or interior to the Gulf and East Coasts, then a preliminary determination could be made of both the size and number of such ports.

As an example, the existing demand of 4 million barrels a day of waterborne petroleum (excluding Venezuelan oil) could be accommodated by two such ports with an approximate throughput of 2 million barrels a day for each port. Each throughput calculation considers, in a very approximate way, a berth occupancy factor (related to waiting delay and in-berth service time), petroleum unloading time, and the number of vessel callings. The estimate of a 2 million barrels per day throughput for a port assumes vessels of 200,000 deadweight tons accommodated by a port having four berths.[1]

Because a port would take a few years to design, approve, and construct, the demand for petroleum for a future period is more germane than existing demand. One of the highest estimates for foreign crude by the National Petroleum Council showed that 14 million barrels per day may be imported by 1985. Under these conditions seven ports of a daily throughput of 2 million barrels may be built. Although supply and demand are both sufficiently dispersed in time and space to prevent all petroleum throughput from funneling through deepwater ports, the calculation may scale some range of port numbers. Under conditions of dispersed demand more ports may be constructed.

If a port were handling 2 million barrels per day every day of the year, its annual imports would about double the total volume of

imported oil to the New York port in 1973. This volume of oil is
comparable to that imported at Rotterdam, which is the largest port
in the world. It is clear that neither the concentration of oil refining
in the United States nor the concentration of consumption in the U.S.
markets would support many ports with a throughput of 2 million
barrels per day.

Near Freeport, Texas, between Corpus Christi and Lake
Charles, there is a sufficient concentration of refining capacity,
about 3.3 million barrels per day, to support such a facility. Near
La Fourche Parish, Louisiana, another deepwater port could reach
the 1.6 million barrel per day refining capacity in Louisiana, and by
pipeline send 2.6 million barrels north to refineries in the mid-West.
SEADOCK expects to handle 1.6 million barrels in 1980 and 1.9
million barrels in 1985. LOOP plans to operate with 1.265 million
barrels in 1980 and 1.875 million barrels in 1985. These facilities
could absorb the 1975 crude oil imports of the entire United States.

With many smaller centers of demand on the East Coast it
would be possible to build much smaller facilities at East Coast sites.
In Bantry Bay, Ireland, a transshipment facility was built with one-
quarter of the capacity mentioned so far, and the Bantry Bay terminal is operated profitably at 200,000 barrels per day--or one-
tenth the size of SEADOCK or LOOP. Even with 4 million barrels
per day throughput on the Gulf Coast, the East Coast could support
additional facilities. About 40 percent of the U.S. petroleum demand
is on the East Coast, with much of the existing refining capacity located between Delaware and New York.

As an exercise in supply and demand analysis, the concept of
tying port throughput capacity to foreign oil imports is useful. This
reasoning follows from the principle that ports would be constructed
only to satisfy future import needs. This simple calculation of port
throughput, and a high and low import demand, yields the range of
deepwater port numbers of two to seven, under the condition that
ports handle 2 million barrels daily. Under conditions of smaller
ports (500,000 barrels per day) designed to serve, for example, a
total volume of 4 million barrels, then eight ports would suffice.
With high volume, onshore refining options would be explored and an
expensive port construction program would be possible. At low
levels the cost of the facility becomes a factor in the siting decision.

It is critical for consideration of deepwater ports to know future demand for oil, and the sources of future supplies. Is it realistic to expect oil imports of 14 million barrels per day by 1985? If
it is realistic, SEADOCK and LOOP might capture about half of this
market. Under these conditions, East Coast deepwater ports would
prove highly desirable to industry.

At much lower levels of demand deepwater ports may attract
oil deliveries from existing ports. Low-demand levels require calculation of diversion of oil to deepwater ports under different conditions of price, concentration of demand centers, and the engineering
limitations on handling a variety of oil products or crude viscosities.
The primary consideration is a forecast range of total imports at
some future date. It would also be well to note Arab intentions in
refinery expansion and possible price shading of refined products
versus crude. The analysis would become quite complicated and
would require a fairly intimate knowledge of the industry.

HISTORICAL CONSUMPTION OF PETROLEUM

As the future consumption of petroleum is a key component of
port planning, past consumption is a reasonable starting point for
analysis. It may be argued that the fourfold increase in crude oil
price and dwindling domestic crude reserves make past consumption
a poor guide to the future. Although true, the departure from the
past may not be as dramatic as some recent forecasts have predicted. About 35 years of increasing reliance on petroleum for
energy is not easily put aside in five or even ten years.

The historical picture, illustrated in Figure 2.1, is one of
consumption increases and higher consumption expenditures. The
only period when consumption actually declined was during World
War II. The decline was accompanied or caused by rationing.
After the war prices increased as shown in the right-hand axis,
from $1.25 to $2.50 per barrel of crude. Since consumption expenditures in the left-hand axis are measured in constant dollars,
the decline in expenditures on petroleum during the war was greater
than the decline in consumption, owing to constant prices.

Subsequent to the war, two periods can be roughly discerned.
From 1945 to 1955 consumption and expenditures increased rapidly.
Owing to the price increases of 1946-47, the expenditure on petroleum (constant dollars) approximately tripled from $3 billion to $9
billion in ten years. Consumption had not let up in the face of much
higher prices. From 1945 to 1955, the nation increased domestic
consumption from more than 700 million barrels to more than 1,300
million barrels.

During the next period of 1955-65, prices stabilized. Prices
reached a peak in about 1958 at a little more than $3 a barrel and
declined or remained steady until the late 1960s.* Consumption

*Ten years of stable prices made for cheap fuel, but the con-
sumption increase was not as great as the previous ten years (1945-55).

FIGURE 2.1

Demand, Price, and Personal Expenditure of Gasoline and Crude Oil in the United States (1929-75)

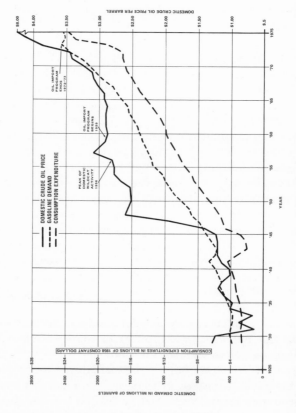

Sources: U.S. Department of Commerce, Survey of Current Business: National Income and Product Accounts of the United States, 1929-1965 (Washington, D.C.: U.S. Government Printing Office, 1966); American Petroleum Institute, Petroleum Facts and Figures, 1971 ed. (Washington, D.C.: American Petroleum Institute, 1973); Oil and Gas Journal 72, no. 30 (July 29, 1974); Oil and Gas Journal 73, no. 30 (July 28, 1975).

continued upward, but not at quite the same rate as the 1945-55 period. By 1965, consumption was a little less than 1,800 barrels. Despite price stability and some slower growth, constant dollar expenditures kept pace with demand.

These periods, 1945-55 and 1955-65, were followed by a trend that mixed elements of both previous periods. Most noticeable is the doubling of domestic crude oil price in 1973-74, reminiscent of the 1946-47 period. Both price increases brought constant dollar expenditures more in line with consumption, as if the price increase were a catch up with inflation. During the war, expenditures, through rationing, declined more acutely than consumption. During the late 1960s and early 1970s consumption was increasing faster than expenditures.

The first dramatic price increase after the war had no effect on consumption. The second price increase of 1973-74 was compounded by a petroleum panic exacerbated by increasing reliance on foreign sources. Gasoline was unavailable for short periods of time in the first months of 1974. Petroleum scarcity combined with a 45 percent increase in the gasoline pump price and other product price increases produced an overall decline in consumption.

Until recently, there was little evidence that demand had much relation to prices. Until 1973-74, the petroleum companies seemed to price oil in order to provide a constant dollar return on every barrel sold, while rapidly increasing the market. The actual pricing developments were and are a great deal more complex. [2]

Some of the significant events during the period of the 1950s and 1960s affected the pattern of consumption. Certainly the Suez crisis and the formation of OPEC led companies to think in terms of stable supply. The outlook for cheap petroleum supply was dwindling at home, while the prospect for cheaply produced foreign crude increased greatly. If these events helped to shape the view that reliable supply and stable prices were principal industry objectives, then the petroleum companies at least secured these objectives through the 1960s. Whatever can be said of the Oil Import Program and the industry during the 1960s, the price was stable and supply was continuous. A principal problem for the industry at that time was that foreign oil was cheaper than domestic. By 1970, the New York harbor delivered price was $1.30 cheaper for foreign oil than domestically produced oil. This problem was translated into an effort to maintain price.

The difference between foreign price and cost, and domestic price compared to foreign price, produced strains on the petroleum industry. At home some companies had few or no overseas operations and were threatened by cheap foreign oil. The large integrated oil companies, on the other hand, could also see no profit in price cutting, and felt the pressure of a few independents with foreign crude who were willing to cut price to increase market share.[3] Although the domestic market was expanding, it had increased in 1955-65 at a slower rate than the previous ten years. Moreover, even if the market could be expanded, the large companies were not willing to shift production overseas at the expense of their own domestic operations.

As a result of a combination of forces, both political and economic, the petroleum industry sought and secured an Oil Import Program. This program, developed under the Department of Interior, set quotas on imported oil. The department allocated licenses to import specific amounts of oil to the industry on an individual company basis. Allocations varied depending upon the formula and regulations. Because imported oil was cheaper than domestic oil to the importer but was sold to the consumer at the same price, the import license holder received a windfall profit. With total imports carefully controlled, however, the overall price to the consumer stabilized. The Oil Import Program was in operation from 1959 to 1973--until the recent past when foreign oil became expensive. With the oil price reasonably stable and with reserve holdings increasing overseas, the major integrated oil companies could pursue the policy of maintaining the price of oil while seeking an expansion of the market.

Prior to 1973, foreign oil was priced lower than domestic oil. In Europe consumers paid their own governments a tax much greater than that paid to producing nations.[4] In the United States there was no such tax, but the supply of cheaper foreign oil was controlled by limiting the amount that could be imported. Import licenses were issued and these licenses were worth the difference between domestic and foreign oil prices--about $1.25 per barrel.[5]

The sources for crude oil have increasingly been foreign producers, as noted in Figure 2.2. The foreign oil share has increased from 19 percent (1960) to 23 percent (1970) to 36 percent (1973). This pattern has not changed significantly since the energy crisis. Consumption (referred to as demand in the figure) declined, but imports maintained their share. Imports continued to be split about equally between refined products and crude oil. With some decline in total consumption it may be expected that international companies prefer to buy crude rather than products unless prices were shaded by foreign refiners.

As noted in Figure 2.3, gasoline is the single largest product derived from a barrel of crude. The Project Independence study indicated that these product mixes may change somewhat as the more price-elastic uses of petroleum, primarily industrial fuel, decline in proportion because of higher prices and the availability of other

FIGURE 2.2

Total Demand and Imports for Petroleum (Crude and Refined Products), 1956–75

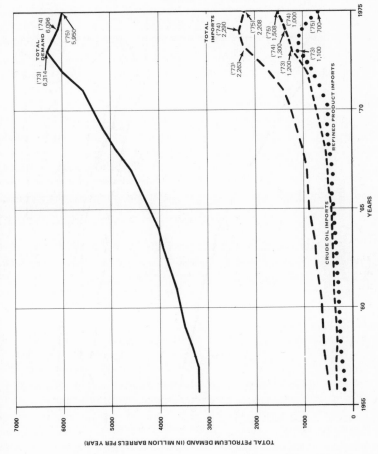

Source: American Petroleum Institute, *Annual Statistical Review*,
1956–1972, Washington, D.C., 1973.
Oil and Gas Journal, *Forecast-Review*, Vol. 73 No. 4,
Jan. 1975 and Vol. 74 No. 4, Jan. 1976.

FIGURE 2.3

Product Demand

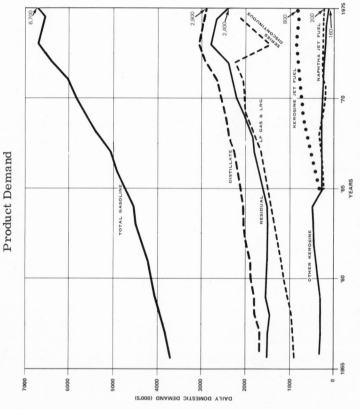

Source: American Petroleum Institute, *Annual Statistical Review,*
1956-1972, Washington, D.C., 1973.
Oil and Gas Journal, *Forecast-Review,* Vol. 73 No. 4,
Jan. 1975 and Vol. 74 No. 4, Jan. 1976.

fuels. The transportation sector, however, is highly dependent upon the internal combustion engine, so that it is not likely that gasoline's share of the product mix will decline relative to other products within the next five to ten years.

SUPPLY AND DEMAND FACTORS

Although the Organization of Petroleum Exporting Countries (OPEC) resents the use of the word "cartel" to describe their organization, they do act as a cartel for the purpose of setting prices and regulating output. Decisions are reached on the basis of consensus, with all the difficulties that organizations for consensual decisions entail. Clearly, oligopolistic pricing is not solely the province of economists, if for no other reason than the factors that hold OPEC together reach beyond economic reasoning to include politics.

Setting this aspect aside, there are other economic factors that affect deepwater port planning. Consumption can be explained in terms of demand, supply, and price. Each of these topics will be discussed in turn. It is also possible to examine these factors in terms of a planning framework, in order to divine what would be necessary to plan for a deepwater port project.

Major uncertainty factors are at least identifiable. The first factor is the current market for deepwater ports in terms of the available volume of petroleum product and crude oil imports that may be diverted to supertankers and deepwater ports. This factor is related to volume, distance, and type of petroleum commodity imported to the United States.

A second factor is the intermediate forecast of petroleum demand for the U.S. market. A collateral issue is an estimate of the extent to which alternative fuels, coal and nuclear power primarily, can dampen long-range petroleum forecasts.

It shall be assumed that existing energy forecasts address this supply issue with sufficient range and depth for an analysis of deepwater port alternatives. In other words, a comprehensive energy study would not be required for the purpose of estimating imported oil demand. Nor is it deemed feasible to estimate cross elasticities between petroleum and other fuels. Moreover, it is explicitly assumed that deepwater ports can be built and operated within a few years; alternative energy sources are assumed to take effect beyond 1985; and a full range of energy options would be available only after 1995.

A third factor is the policy objective of national self-sufficiency or hemispheric self-sufficiency by 1985. Aside from a problem of

definition, this factor is limited by domestic oil production possibilities. This factor also depends upon energy conservation. Energy
conservation is both a short- and long-term option. It is possible to
reduce consumption, and over a longer period improve capital pur-
chases for energy efficiency. In time technological innovation becomes important, as well as the turnover in capital assets.

A fourth factor is the price of oil, and the long-run demand-
price elasticity. This factor relates to both national self-sufficiency
and energy conservation.

A fifth factor is the capacity of existing transportation facilities
and the need for additional refining capacity. Related to the production process and transportation networks is the extent to which
hemispheric production will move offshore. Offshore production
will entail transport network investment that may be planned in
coordination with port facilities for imported oil. Offshore production requires either tankers or pipelines linked to onshore terminals,
pipelines, and refineries. Offshore production can increase the
need for terminal facilities. The five factors can be summarized
under the headings of domestic energy supplies, oil import demand,
oil price, government oil policy, and transport network considerations.

DOMESTIC ENERGY SUPPLIES

Under conditions of stable prices, demand is forecast and price
indicates how the market may be cleared. Under conditions of price
fluctuation, demand is forecast under different price assumptions.
Given the uncertainties of whether crude oil is $6, $8, $10, or $16
a barrel, domestic energy supply becomes a more stable indication
of the short-term future than a demand forecast. In the short run,
only certain fuels can be expanded rapidly to meet demand. It is
questionable whether total energy supply and demand forecasts are
needed every time an oil price change is announced. In the short
run, there is little that can be done in response to high prices except
to conserve fuel. In the long run, an overall energy policy should
describe which fuel supplies ought to be expanded and the incentives
that will assure such expansion.

A graphic picture of the inability to close the supply/demand
gap is illustrated in Figure 2.4. As presented, the U.S. petroleum
situation is viewed in light of reserves, production, and future
petroleum discovery. The U.S. production of oil has shown rapid
expansion since the late nineteenth century. The area under the
curve indicates that 100×10^9 barrels have been produced. This
curve may be compared to demand and consumption expenditures in

FIGURE 2.4

U.S. Petroleum Reserves
(proved, undiscovered, and ultimate recovery)

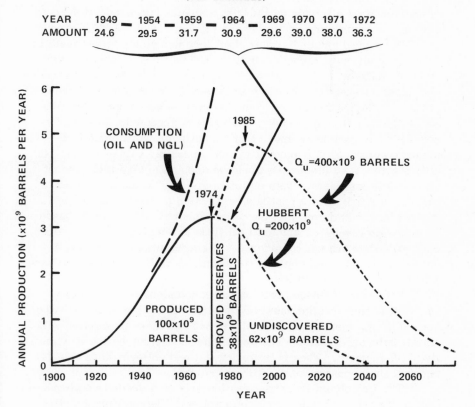

PROVED RESERVES (10⁹ BARRELS)							
YEAR	1949	1954	1959	1964	1969	1970	1971	1972
AMOUNT	24.6	29.5	31.7	30.9	29.6	39.0	38.0	36.3

- - - - - - REPRESENTS TWO ESTIMATES OF ULTIMATE RECOVERY (PRODUCED, PROVED AND UNDISCOVERED)

Source: R. R. Berg, C. L. Calhoun, and J. C. Whiting, "Prognosis for Expanded U.S. Production of Crude Oil," Science 184 (April 19, 1974): 330-36.

Figure 2.1. Despite this increase in production, consumption has
moved ahead of production, indicating the supply/demand gap noted
in Figure 2.4. Proven reserves were estimated at 38 x 10^9 barrels
in 1971, which would take the United States through 1985 with reasonably stable production.* In order to indicate the history of such a
reserve position, the history of these estimates is shown at the top
of the figure. Since 1954 such proven reserves were reasonably
stable except for the 1970 Alaskan oil discovery. Prior to 1954 reserves increased.

Since more oil discoveries are continually made, an estimate
of undiscovered oil made by Hubbert indicates how production could
decline but remain important beyond the year 2000. Adding production, discovered and undiscovered oil together yields an estimate by
Hubbert of ultimate recovery of 200 x 10^9 barrels. Hubbert's estimate of undiscovered oil, which used to be considered low, is reasonably close to industry forecasts and the National Academy of Sciences'.[6] The estimate of proven reserves is based upon good evidence, but prediction is risky, even if it is accepted. The "undiscovered" category is no more than an estimate based upon frag-
mentary evidence. To account for such possible variance, the total
ultimate recovery (domestic) could be doubled to take into account
all possible forecasts. This estimate yields a dotted line 400 x 10^9
barrels that indicates a continued expansion of production to 1985.
It must be remembered that the oil producer's calculation is based
upon proven reserves, and until oil finds are moved into the proven
category, they are not considered. If consumption is trended, it
outpaces even the most optimistic estimates of U.S. (continental and
offshore) supply possibilities.

From the evidence, two logical conclusions may be drawn.
One is that conservation must be practiced to reduce demand. The
second is that there is no possibility that increased production will
satisfy growing demand. The petroleum industry sees the inevitability of oil imports. The environmentalist and policymakers see the
necessity for conservation. All can be right.

The petroleum industry sees imports as a predictive phenomenon rather than an objective public policy. The environmentalist
views imports in light of disruptive effects, compared to other
energy-production programs. Economic and foreign-policy analysts
are anxious not to be dependent upon foreign oil.

All of the factors related to supply tend to indicate that domestic production cannot, by itself, eliminate imports. If the nation

---

*Current estimates due to price increases raise proven re-
serves to 44 x 10^9 barrels.

satisfied its energy growth by rapidly increasing domestic oil production, then by 1985 there would be a rapid decline in production.
The economic and environmental consequences of such domestic oil
expansion may be unreasonable, and even if it is a reasonable policy,
the political will is lacking to eliminate imports by this means.

Finding oil at home has declined in volume and in the rate of
success.[7] About one-third of the domestic oil found is from offshore fields. It may be useful to compare various future domestic
production estimates under different domestic price conditions.
Nevertheless, as recently as 1972 the domestic producers were not
unhappy with a crude oil price of $4.00. At $3.30 the industry had
doubts about expansion, but with domestic oil at $8.00 or more the
incentive for production should be present. Exploration and drilling
have increased, but this has not yet shown up in reserves or production increases.

Until reserves begin to increase there is little incentive to
produce greater quantities of oil. The graph indicates that "probable" reserves represent a limited number of years' production. If
more oil is not found, the oil industry must weigh whether future
prices will reward stretching out production. In other words, the
present price is an incentive to produce more oil if more oil is found.
If more oil is not found, then future price becomes important.

If the supply side shows that imports are inevitable, what about
the demand side? To some extent demand can be approached obliquely
through past estimates of future consumption. This oblique approach
is useful, because energy studies of the past saw future consumption
in terms of economic forces that assumed cheap and stable petroleum
prices. These studies also assumed that supply would be continuous,
and oil imports would be the easiest alternative in making up the gap
between domestically consumed and produced energy. These past
projections are useful to indicate how stable and cheap petroleum is
viewed in a growing economy.

HISTORICAL PERSPECTIVE

Past estimates of future consumption have ignored the effects
of price upon demand. Whatever the "real" explanatory variables,
price was clearly not a factor in determining the demand for petroleum. Prices over the years have not changed much since World
War II. The 1960s were a particularly stable period. For example,
in 1957 the price for domestic crude rose above $3.00, but did not
increase to $3.00 again until 1967. Again, between 1960 and 1970,
the price of Louisiana crude rose from $3.02 to $3.67. This 20
percent increase in ten years made oil a bargain. Since prices were

so stable, it was possible to overlook the effect of price. Many demand forecasts ignored the possibility of demand under different
prices simply because no one expected prices to change much.

In the past the best single indicator of demand was the Gross
National Product (GNP) or other measures of national product or income. One critic of the Ford energy study used Figure 2.5 to
point out that economic growth and energy demand are closely linked.

> In the Technical Fix and more especially in the
> Zero Energy Growth scenarios, the Energy Policy
> Project has assumed that the growth in energy
> usage and the growth in the nation's economy can be
> uncoupled. I consider these assertions totally un-
> supported and unsubstantiated by the fact. There
> is a wealth of data which substantiates the widely
> accepted contention that growth in energy usage
> and the growth in the economy are inextricably
> linked. [8]

The problem with this wealth of data is the stable prices on
which it is built. The opposite is also true--a model indicating the
ability to greatly reduce demand infers this from price data that is beyond the range of past experience. There is simply not a representative time series upon which to build a good simulation of price
changes for petroleum.

Another way of presenting the historical picture is to examine
past projections. Based upon projections compiled by Robert R.
Nathan, two series of projections are presented. [9] The first series
is a compilation of forecasts made from 1963-68, noted by small
squares in Figure 2.6. The second series (in circles) is also projected to 1980 and 1985, but the projections were made after 1968.
As a group, the post-1968 projections are slightly higher. The
demand for petroleum was growing at an increasing rate during the
1968-73 period than in the period prior to 1968. With a few exceptions, all the growth-rate projections for petroleum clustered between 2 percent and 4 percent per annum. These projections are
reasonably close but slightly lower than projections in national
product during the same period.

One central question is how much can price alone dampen the
demand for petroleum. The results from the model presented later
indicate that zero petroleum growth is a reasonable expectation.

The interdependence between economic growth and petroleum
prices is evident in the economic downturn in the U.S. economy in
1974. Constant dollar GNP declined by 2 percent from 1976 and
1974. This fact alone would reduce normal growth in consumption

FIGURE 2.5

The Interdependence of Energy and Economic Growth

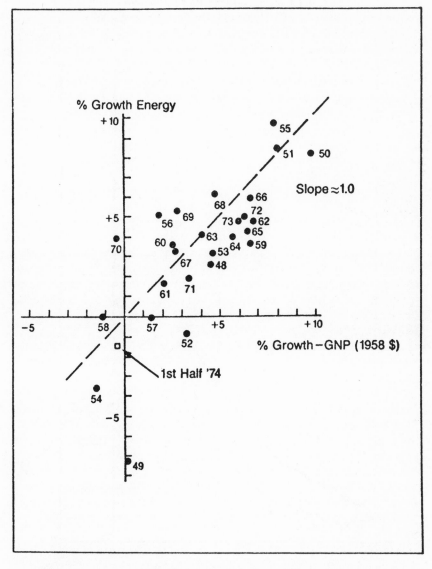

Note: The percentage growth in GNP closely parallels the percentage growth in energy.

Source: Commentary by Donald C. Burnham in Energy Policy Project of the Ford Foundation, A Time to Choose (Cambridge, Mass.: Ballinger, 1974), p. 368.

FIGURE 2.6

Demand for Petroleum Products and
Crude Oil Domestic Production
(1956 to 1972; projections to 1980 and 1985)

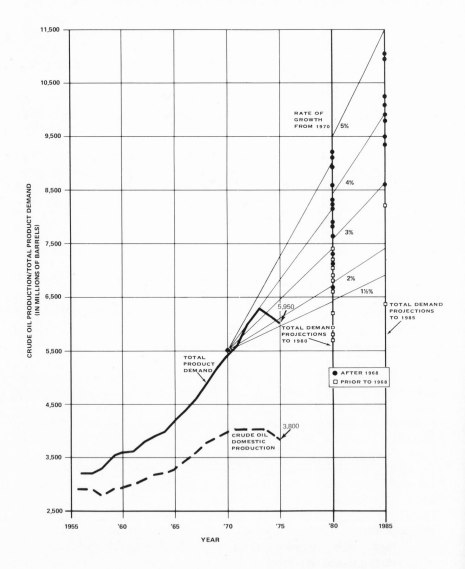

Source: Robert R. Nathan Associates, U.S. Deepwater Port
Study, 5 vols. (Springfield, Va.: National Technical Information
Service, 1972), 2:99-113.

of petroleum. Another facet of this interdependence is the amount of GNP loss attributable to higher petroleum prices. A recent study found that about half of the 1974 shortfall in output and employment was due to the rise in oil prices.[10]

This interdependence between energy and economy is difficult to model, and econometric models are based on past prices that did not fluctuate greatly. To argue that the trends cannot "bend" greatly is not naive, and perhaps less naive than a model that purports to capture the complexity of the economy. Econometric models, however, do test the conventional wisdom. Both Robert Nathan and the Arthur D. Little study assumed a greater level of imports than are now expected with much higher prices. The question is how much less petroleum consumption growth there will be, and can the United States reduce imports below current levels of 6 million barrels per day.

By 1980 the Robert Nathan study projected 8.9 million barrels per day of petroleum imports and Arthur D. Little estimated from 5.8 to 8.2 million barrels. As noted in Table 2.1, the two studies disagreed about the destination of these imports. Clearly, most of the petroleum would be ultimately consumed in the East, but the Arthur D. Little study had to consider for impact analysis which ports the petroleum would enter. Consequently, the differences on these estimates are more apparent than real. The Little study evaluated impacts in terms of where the petroleum was imported and refined and not where the petroleum was consumed.

THE IMPACT OF PRICES ON DEMAND

Higher prices affect demand and the kinds of oil conservation measures that are sought by policy. Prices may be the only effective policy instrument in achieving conservation, despite often-stated intent by government officials to use other levers. Historically, the domestic crude oil price has been higher than the foreign price. This difference reflects the vastly unequal costs of production. Typically, foreign oil prices have borne no relationship to foreign oil-production costs. The costs may be as little as ten cents a barrel and the price as high as $12 a barrel.

The history of price change is noted in Table 2.2, where substantive changes can be outlined. The relative difference in foreign and domestic price is noted along with the change in price levels.

The immediate impact of these price changes was to dampen the growth in consumption. By May of 1974, the Federal Energy Office estimated that the averaged "old oil" and "exempt oil" domestic crude price was $7.15 and actual imported oil price was $10.42. These estimates and gasoline price increases are noted in Table 2.3.

TABLE 2.1

Waterborne Petroleum Imports: East and Gulf Coasts
(million barrels per calendar day)

Study Source	Petroleum Type	1980 Estimate			1985 Estimate		
		District I[a]	District II–IV[b]	Total	District I	District II–IV	Total
Robert R. Nathan Associates	Crude	2.0	3.0	5.0			
	Residual	3.0	--	3.0		No Forecast	
	Other product	0.9	--	0.9			
	Total	5.9	3.0	8.9			

		East Coast		Gulf Coast	Total		East Coast		Gulf Coast	Total	
		Low Level	High Level				Low Level	High Level			
Arthur D. Little	Crude	1.1	3.5	4.7	5.8	8.2	1.6	5.1	6.8	8.4	11.9

[a]District I is the East Coast from Maine to Florida and includes Vermont and West Virginia.

[b]District II–IV includes all other states except the West Coast, Alaska, and Hawaii. Canadian imports estimated at 1.7 million barrels per day for this district.

Sources: Robert R. Nathan Associates, U.S. Deepwater Port Study, 5 vols. (Springfield, Va.: National Technical Information Service, 1972), 2: 73–74; Arthur D. Little, Potential Onshore Effects of Deepwater Oil Terminal-Related Industrial Development, 5 vols. (Springfield, Va.: National Technical Information Service, 1973), 1: 1–4.

TABLE 2.2

Comparative Prices of Crude Oil
(dollars per barrel)

Date	Arabian Light[a]	South Louisiana[b]	West Texas Sour[b]
1960	1.80	3.02	2.79
1965	1.80	3.11	2.83
1970	1.80	3.63	3.31
1971	2.29 (June)	3.63	3.37
1972	2.48 (Jan. 20)	3.67	3.37
1973	5.12 (Oct. 16)[d]	4.27 (Oct. 15)[c]	4.12 (Oct. 15)[c]
1974	11.65 (Jan. 1)	5.27 (Jan. 15)[c]	5.12 (Jan. 15)[c]
1975	11.25 (Aug. 1975)[e]	4.93-5.35 (Aug.)[c]	4.78-5.20 (Aug.)[c]

[a]Posted prices Arabian Light 34° gravity crude FOB Ras Tanura. Does not include discounts. For a discussion see M. A. Adelman, The World Petroleum Market (Baltimore: Johns Hopkins University Press, 1972), Chapter 6.

[b]Lowest price paid at end of year exclusive of local port or other government charges.

[c]Under price controls. Uncontrolled production that was a small percentage was soon to rise to worldwide levels. Uncontrolled production estimated at 40 percent in 1975 with an average price of $12.07.

[d]The price on October 1 was $3.01.

[e]Does not include about $2.00 oil import fee. Estimated price through customs was $12.43 in June 1975. Also does not reflect discounts estimated at 7 percent. Actual price estimated at $10.41 plus fee for a total of $12.43.

Sources: Platt's Oilgram Price Service, Platt's Oilgram, 50th ed. (New York: McGraw-Hill, 1974); Foster Associates, Inc., Energy Prices: 1960-1973 (Cambridge, Mass.: Ballinger, 1974), pp. 16-18; Platt's Oilgram Price Service, Platt's Oilgram (New York: McGraw-Hill, 1975), August 15 and September 4, 1975.

TABLE 2.3

Average and Typical Petroleum Prices
(nationwide)

	1968	1970	1973	1974
Gasoline (cents per gallon)[a]				
Pump price	0.34	0.36	0.39	0.52 (April 1974)
Price excluding taxes[b]	0.23	0.25	0.27	0.41
Crude oil (dollars per barrel)				
Domestic	3.08	3.23	3.87	7.15
Foreign	2.20[d]	2.20[d]	2.59[c] (January 1)	10.42[c]
			5.12 (October 16)	

[a]Gasoline costs from U.S. Federal Highway Administration.

[b]Fifty-five cities average price.

[c]Prices are at well, which does not include delivery. Average price estimated by Federal Energy Office for May 1974.

[d]Estimated by M. A. Adelman for 1969 at $1.20 to produce. Includes foreign taxes plus approximately $1.00 per barrel for transportation.

Sources: U.S. Federal Highway Administration, "Operating Cost of an Automobile" (1970, 1972, 1974); Platt's Oilgram Price Service, Platt's Oilgram (New York: McGraw-Hill, 1969); American Petroleum Institute, Petroleum Facts and Figures (Washington, D.C., 1969); U.S. Dept. of Commerce, Survey of Current Business (Washington, D.C., 1969-74); M. A. Adelman, The World Petroleum Market (Baltimore: Johns Hopkins University Press, 1972); U.S. Congress, Senate Interior and Insular Affairs, Oil and Gas Import Issues, 93rd Cong., 1st session, 1972, Parts I-III.

Using typical price figures it is possible to estimate the impact of these prices on demand. Consumption declined from 17.25 million barrels per day to 16.91 million barrels per day nationwide.* These declines reflected both the interruption in supply as well as price increases. During 1973-74, GNP declined in real terms by about 2 percent.

A SIMPLE DEMAND MODEL

A simple model was chosen to evaluate how demand changes with price. The model was chosen for its minimum data requirements. The object was to estimate price/demand elasticity given some reasonable assumptions about income elasticity. The long- and short-term income elasticities were taken from the work of Verlager and Sheehan.[11] In the exponential form the model can be estimated by the following equation:

$$Q_t = Q_o \left[P_1/P_o \right]^b \left[\frac{Y_1}{Y_o} \right]^d$$

The principal function of the model is to estimate consumption for a distant period, but not so distant as to require cross-elasticity estimates with coal or natural gas.

Applied to 1973-74, an income elasticity of 0.6 was assumed. Table 2.4 shows these data yielded estimated price elasticities of -.13 for all petroleum products and -.22 for gasoline. This estimate is similar to those found in other studies already cited.

By 1975 the crude oil "exempt" from price controls had increased to $12.07 per barrel, which combined with an "old oil" price of $5.35 yields a domestic price of $8.04. Foreign oil price was higher in 1975 due to the oil import fee introduced in the beginning of the year. The estimated foreign oil price is $12.43 through May. The volume weighted average for 1975 is about $9.66 per barrel in contrast to $8.00 per barrel in 1974.

With higher prices in 1975, consumption continued to decline to about 16.3 million barrels. A part of this decline can be attributed to still higher prices, but another part reflects the lagged adjustment to 1974 price increases. Unlike 1974, the economy showed increased

---

*Later data adjusted to 16.7 million barrels in 1974, which is not reflected in Table 2.4.

TABLE 2.4

Demand/Price Elasticity

(million barrels of oil daily equivalent)

Consumption, 1973[a] (million barrels per day equivalent)	Gross National Product (1973–74)[b] (billions of dollars)	Percent Change in Price, 1973–74[c]	Consumption, 1974	Price/Demand Elasticity, 1973–74 (current dollars)
Total consumption 17,250	−2.1% (constant)	64	16,910	−.13
Gasoline consumption 7,121	7.9% (current)	33	6,875	−.22
		Total Petroleum Demand Elasticity Based on Gasoline Price Increases		−.21

[a]Total demand based on Oil and Gas Journal (July 1974) for the period January 1973–74. Gasoline demand from Federal Highway Administration (FHWA) news release, March 28, 1975, for October 1973 to October 1974.

[b]All estimates are based on current dollars. Calculations based upon income elasticity of 0.6 (or a one-year change).

[c]Based upon 28¢ gasoline and 11¢ tax in 1972 (39¢); and 41¢ gasoline and 11¢ tax (52¢) for 1974. Total demand is based upon a domestic crude oil price increase from $3.87 per barrel in 1973 to $6.33 per barrel in 1974. Survey of Current Business is the source of prices for gasoline and crude; gasoline price is the 55¢ city average price for the year. Crude oil price is the Oklahoma-Kansas price for year, except 1974 where price was reported for March.

Sources: Petroleum Publishing Co., Oil and Gas Journal (Tulsa: July 1974); FHWA news release, Washington, D.C., March 28, 1975; U.S. Department of Commerce, Survey of Current Business (Washington, D.C.: U.S. Government Printing Office, 1974).

national product in 1975. Application of the equation to 1973-75
price and GNP changes would indicate higher price elasticity estimates after a two-year period.

INCOME ELASTICITY

Income elasticity for a three-year period was considered to be
near unity in the Data Resources, Inc. (DRI) study of gasoline. If
gasoline were considered near the middle of the elasticity range for
petroleum products, then this estimate might apply to all petroleum.
To the extent that a growth relationship in energy and GNP can be inferred from Figure 2.2, an income elasticity of 1.0 is plausible.
Both income and price elasticity tend to increase over time, but for
different reasons. Price elasticity increases because substitution
of fuels becomes possible. Income elasticity reflects demand for
increased capital goods as well as higher level of output for final
demand.

It may well be true that in the past the high income elasticity
of petroleum reflected the growing output from an industrial economy.
As fuel substitution becomes possible in the future, price elasticity
may increase and thereby dampen consumption. As petroleum becomes scarce, the income elasticity may remain high due to the
specialized uses it can be put to in a developed and affluent economy.
Consequently, petroleum may become both a more valuable and less
dominant fuel in the future. Petroleum may become more closely
tied to the price fluctuations and growth swings of the economy.

FUTURE PRICE POSSIBILITIES

Future prices are uncertain and cannot be estimated based
upon past prices. As noted in Table 2.5, the Project Independence
study estimated prices at $4.00, $7.00, $10.34, and $13.68. For
the purpose of policy considerations, the study discussed only $7.00
and $11.00 options. The Ford study assumed $10.40 price (assuming a $6.33 base) for crude oil and faster rates of price increases
for products. [12]

The Project Independence assumption about prices in their
"policy options" may be faulty. By May of 1974 the Federal Energy
Office reported a volume weighted price of $8.00, reflecting the
domestic price of $7.15 and a foreign oil price of $10.42. By May
of 1975, with a $2.00 oil import fee the volume weighted price was
estimated at $9.66 for all petroleum.

TABLE 2.5

Data Resources, Inc.: Econometric Model--Price Assumptions
(price and own elasticities)

Fuels	1973	1980 Alternative Price				1985 Alternative Price				Own Elasticity	
		1	2	3	4	1	2	3	4	Short Run	Long Run 1985
Crude (dollars per barrel)	4.00	4.00	7.00	10.34	13.68	4.00	7.00	10.86	14.71		
Gasoline (dollars per gallon)	0.40		.42	.50	.58		.42	.50	.59	-.2	-.76
Distillate fuel (dollars per barrel)	5.58		9.14	12.48	15.82		8.68	12.53	16.38	--	-.35 to -.46 (T) -.94 to -1.4 (I) -.64 to -.67 (H)
Residual fuel (dollars per barrel)	4.58		7.00	10.34	13.68		7.00	10.86	14.71	--	-.19 (T) -1.38 to 1.86 (I) -.34 to -.38 (H)

Note: T = Transportation Sector; H = Household Sector; and I = Industrial Sector.

Source: Project Independence, Federal Energy Administration (Washington 1974), Appendix A11-1, Table A11-1, p. 60, and Table A11-9, p. 69.

If old oil is "unfrozen" then domestic oil would rise to foreign price levels. Immediately the price would rise to about $11.00. Policy options limited to $7 and $11 oil prices may be wishful thinking in order to illustrate a manageable situation, but it is not a reflection of the prices oil may reach.

MODEL PARAMETER ASSUMPTIONS-- LONG-TERM APPLICATION

The model described on p. 35 can be used with both long-term and short-term price elasticities. Several price assumptions are used. Both the DRI and the Houthakker and Taylor studies have estimated the short-term gasoline price elasticity in the range of -.2 and the long-term price elasticity near -.5.[13]

In performing the econometric work for Project Independence, DRI estimated a somewhat higher price elasticity to 1985. In that study the long-run gasoline price elasticity was -.76, as shown in Table 2.5. Other petroleum products in the transportation and residential sectors were assumed to be less elastic than gasoline. In the industrial sector, distillate and residual fuel are estimated to be more elastic than gasoline. Overall gasoline was no more elastic than the other petroleum products. Given that gasoline is about half of all product demand, the overall estimate from -.5 to -.76 is close to a volume-weighted, total-product demand.

Using the model and a reasonable set of long-range price and income elasticities, it becomes possible to calculate future petroleum consumption. A few illustrations show how a low growth future becomes plausible. For example, real GNP increasing at 3.5 percent, price elasticity at -.5, and income elasticity of 1.0 yields a 2 percent annual decline in petroleum consumption by 1980. The actual figures are 17.25 million barrels daily in 1973 to 15.2 million barrels daily in 1980. Such a future would probably mean less imports than current levels. If all the above conditions took place over a 12-year period to 1985, then petroleum consumption would decline to 15.6 million barrels.

The difficulty is that small changes in the assumed values make quite a difference in the results. For example, low price elasticity (-.2) and higher income growth (4 percent) will yield a consumption estimate of 19.6 million barrels by 1980. This is nearly a 2 percent increase in petroleum per annum, representing modest growth.

Estimates can range all around the ballpark, depending upon one's elasticity estimates. Quite clearly a more elegant model can slow down these interactions and constrain the variance of forecasts. Often it is difficult to know when such elegance is expressing actual

economic processes, or whether it is a computational device to keep
the model's results within acceptable bounds of judgmental accuracy.

No growth and actual declines in petroleum consumption are
quite plausible under a variety of reasonable assumptions. Looking
back to Figure 2.2, it also appears that GNP growth without petroleum consumption increases is an unlikely prospect. Alternative
energy supplies will not be available soon enough to exert substitution effects. Clearly this simple model may be faulty, but a better
model will require more assumptions. Perhaps the most convincing
argument for reduced petroleum consumption is the ability to conserve given that the United States has grown wasteful over the years
with cheap energy, particularly petroleum. The conventional wisdom
that the economy cannot grow without increased consumption may be
faulty; it may also be true that an effective conservation policy by
government is unnecessary as long as prices remain high and are
assumed to remain high in the future.

COMPARISON OF IMPORT FORECASTS

Regardless of specific forecasts with their different assumptions, it is possible to estimate imports from a range of growth
rates. At no growth (0 percent), at 2 percent, and at 3.5 percent
growth an estimate of imports can be made. Such an estimate in
Table 2.6 shows a combination of domestic production and consumption forecasts. Production assumptions are based upon National
Petroleum Council figures. For the purpose of impact analysis in
the next chapter, the highest waterborne estimate is used--8.0
million barrels per day.

A waterborne import estimate depends upon supply, demand,
Canadian imports, and the allocation between crude and refined
products. This latter consideration is discussed in Chapter 4 in
connection with specific port sites, the need to import residual oil,
and demand in sectors of the United States. The translation of total
imports into waterborne imports is shown in the notes to Table 2.6.
Although the 8.0 million barrel range is used in the analysis, a 6.0
million barrel import estimate might be considered more likely.
The 6.0 million barrel estimate assumes that either overall consumption will increase at 2 percent with a modest domestic production increase, or consumption will be less than 2 percent with fairly
constant domestic production.

In any case the range of estimates can be compared to the
Project Independence assumptions. Project Independence econometric treatment indicates considerably more variation than their
summary analysis would indicate on the basis of $7.00 and $11.00

TABLE 2.6

U.S. Petroleum Supply/Consumption
(millions of barrels of daily oil equivalent)

	1970	1973	1980[a]			1985[a]		
			0 Percent Growth	2 Percent Growth	3.5 Percent Growth	0 Percent Growth	2 Percent Growth	3.5 Percent Growth
Total consumption	14.7	17.25	17.7	19.7	22.0	17.7	21.9	26.0
Total production (estimates for 1980–85, National Petroleum Council)	11.3	11.05	13.6[b]	13.6[b]	13.8[c]	15.5[c]	15.5[b]	16.9[c]
Total imports	3.4	6.2[d]	4.1	6.1	8.2	2.2	6.4	9.1
Total waterborne (imports excluding Canada)	2.7	5.1	low[e] 3.0	5.0	7.1	1.1	5.3	8.0
			high[f] 2.2	4.2	6.3	0	4.0	6.7

[a]The 3.5 percent growth is the average forecast of 20 energy studies. The National Petroleum Council has predicted (1973) a 3.8 percent increase for 1970–85. A 2 percent growth assumes an elasticity of .2 at the price change of $3.87 to $8.00 per barrel. The higher growth rate requires a decline in real prices.

[b]Based upon Case I of National Petroleum Council's U.S. Energy Outlook, where Case I requires a price of $4.90 per barrel and drilling rate of 5.5 percent per year. Recent drilling rate (1974) has recorded an 18 percent increase.

[c]Includes Case I assumptions (National Petroleum Council) for synthetic crude and coal synthetic crude. No synthetic crude or coal synthetic crude production was assumed for zero percent growth or 2 percent growth alternatives.

[d]Based upon actual imports first half of 1974 estimated by the Federal Energy Office.

[e]Assumes constant imports from Canada at 1.1 million barrels per day.

[f]Assumes 2:1 ratio of total developable Canadian hydrocarbons to U.S. imports. The National Petroleum Council estimates hydrocarbon that can be produced in Canada at 1.6 million barrels per day (1970), 2.3 million (1975), 3.7 million (1980), and 4.7 million (1985). U.S. imports were 41 percent of these estimates for 1970 and 48 percent in 1974 (at developable of 2.3MM b/d).

Sources: National Petroleum Council, U.S. Energy Outlook (December 1972), p. 57; Institute for Water Resources, U.S. Deepwater Port Study II: 73, Table 13; and "Midyear Report," Oil and Gas Journal (July 29, 1974): 130.

crude oil future. From the various tables regarding supply and consumption, the import needs can be calculated from Project Independence. Table 2.7 shows by 1985 4 million barrels to 12 million barrels per day imports under the $7.00 and $11.00 prices. These import futures actually become negative (exports) if accelerated development is considered. The Federal Energy Office (FEO) supply forecasts are more bullish than pre-energy crisis National Petroleum Council's most optimistic (Case I) estimate.[14] The 1980 supply (domestic production) case is much closer to current output, but still represents higher than current supply, even with $4.00 crude price.

The Project Independence estimates assume that supply (domestic production) can be increased sufficiently with $11.00 to reduce oil imports. With conservation and $11.00 oil, consumption can remain at 1973 levels. With accelerated development and conservation, the study assumes that imports can be eliminated by 1985.

The Project Independence estimates on accelerated development are a little suspect considering Hubbert's estimates of supply. In ten years, $11.00 oil nearly doubles supply. Accelerated development as a policy assumes finding more oil. If more oil is not found, the United States must rely on foreign sources after 1985 or have alternative energy supplies available. It may not be prudent to seek such domestic oil production unless a lot more oil is found to sustain production after 1985. As shown in Table 2.8, zero imports and not just zero growth is considered feasible without accelerated development. The Ford study is one example.

With imports at 6 million barrels per day (Ford study, high fossil fuel or nuclear supply), imports do not increase. Under their technical-fix scenario, zero imports are estimated by 1985. The M.I.T. study and Project Independence also concur in zero imports, but differ in time frame. There is, however, little evidence of effective conservation, which appears to be a prime ingredient for these lowest groups of estimates. Moreover, the Ford study tolerates higher imports of oil in the short term, because of their environmental concern about the cost of switching to coal and offshore leasing. Only an objective of domestic production increase, at any cost, is really consistent with zero imports.

The writer's estimates and these post-energy crisis studies can be compared to earlier estimates on deepwater ports. These earlier estimates are the waterborne petroleum import forecasts presented in the Arthur D. Little study and the Robert R. Nathan study. As these earlier studies did not anticipate the energy crisis, the comparisons are more informative about the petroleum movement than as indications of likely total petroleum imports.

TABLE 2.7

Project Independence
(million of barrels per day/dollars per barrel of crude)

| | Price (dollars) | | | | | |
| | 1980 | | | 1985 | | |
	4	7	11	4	7	11
Demand						
A. Case I: Business as usual	--	20.6	17.4	--	23.9	19.1
Case II: BAU with conservation	--	19.0	16.2	--	21.2	16.9
B. Case I: Accelerated development with conservation	--	18.7	16.1	--	20.6	17.9
Case II: AD without conservation	--	20.4	17.1	--	23.7	19.2
Supply						
A. Case I: Business as usual	9.8	11.1	12.2	9.8	11.9	15.0
B. Case II: Accelerated development	11.1	12.9	13.5	11.6	16.9	20.0
Petroleum imports						
A.1. Business as usual (supply demand)	--	9.5	5.2	--	12.0	4.1
A.2. BAU S/D with conservation	--	7.9	4.0	--	9.3	1.9
B.1. Accelerated development with conservation	--	5.8	2.6	--	3.7	-2.1
B.2. Accelerated development without conservation	--	7.5	3.6	--	6.8	-0.8

Source: Federal Energy Administration, Project Independence (November 1974), Appendix Tables P1-P-12, pp. 33-44, and Table II-8, p. 81.

TABLE 2.8

Petroleum Imports--Post-Energy Crisis
Comparison of Estimates
(barrels per day)

		1980	1985
Author's estimates			
Prices	Consumption		
$8.00/1980; $11.00/1985	0% growth	4.1	2.2
Less than $8.00/1980, and $11.00/1985	2% growth	6.1	6.4
Less than $8.00/1980, and less than $11.00/1985	3.5% growth (with National Petroleum Council Case I supply) All cases	8.2	9.1
Ford study (historical growth) Exploring energy choices			
High imports		8.5	9.4
High supply (fossil fuel)		5.2	2.8
High nuclear supply		6.6	5.2
Ford study (technical fix)			
Base		4.7	0
Low nuclear		--	1.9
High nuclear		--	-1.8
National Academy of Engineering		--	0
M.I.T. judgmental model (at $11.00 a barrel oil)		0	--
M.I.T. econometric model (at $11.00 a barrel oil)		0	--
Federal Energy Administration Accelerated development			
with conservation	$7.00 oil	5.8	3.7
	$11.00 oil	2.6	-2.1
Business as usual without conservation	$7.00 oil	9.5	12.0
	$11.00 oil	5.2	4.1

Source: From Tables F-2 and F-8, Appendix A-III, p. 18 and p. 24, and converted from BTUs at 5.8 million per barrel in Federal Energy Administration, Project Independence (November 1974).

It is clear that all the Nathan and Little estimates are high for both 1980 and 1985. With 3.7 million barrel daily imports as a median 1985 estimate for the studies in Table 2.8 (Ford, Federal Energy Administration, M.I.T., and Academy of Engineering), then the 8.2 b/d to 11.9 b/d deepwater port study range is too high. Nevertheless, such higher estimates are useful for impact assessment. In Chapter 4, the 9.1 million barrel level is used (8.0 million barrels waterborne) for assessing refinery decisions. This higher level is not a prediction.

CONCLUSION

The effect of the high price of oil is to reduce the demand for imports. Zero growth is feasible under a number of reasonable price and elasticity assumptions. Zero imports have been estimated by a number of studies.

The simple model presented in this chapter yields zero growth with price elasticity of -.5 and current prices; there may be some decline in consumption under these conditions. The model applied to 1973-74 tends to support conclusions on short-term petroleum and gasoline price elasticities.

Despite these zero growth options, even a 2 percent growth in petroleum will result in much lower import estimates than what the Arthur D. Little and Robert R. Nathan studies indicate. Waterborne imports may be about half of these studies based upon the post-energy crisis consensus. At 2 percent petroleum growth and a modest domestic production increase, 6.0 million barrels per day imports are likely.

Lower demand increases the opportunity to concentrate investment at likely existing deepwater port sites. Despite the greater East Coast than Gulf Coast market demand, the decision to construct a port may be delayed indefinitely. One possibility is the construction of smaller terminals designed to serve only existing East Coast refinery locations. Siting would be just as much a problem with a small 200,000 barrel per day operation as with a much larger facility. It is less likely, however, that such terminals will attract refineries nearby.

The demand elasticity estimates would lead to zero petroleum imports or zero petroleum growth (zero percent) imports under a number of conditions. The estimates made by the Ford and Project Independence studies are inclined to be overstated, but low petroleum growth is likely. These estimates tend to support the conclusion that imports will remain near existing levels over the next ten years. The United States may be able to support a few (less than three) ports as a consequence. The exception to this conclusion is where a deepwater port is sited in Maine in natural harbors as a low-cost transshipment terminal. Such a terminal would compete with Caribbean and Canadian sites where transshipment is also feasible.

NOTES

1. Calculations were based upon the Institute for Water Resources report. Robert R. Nathan Associates, U.S. Deepwater Port Study: Physical Coast and Port Characteristics and Selected Deepwater Port Alternatives, 5 vols. (Springfield, Va.: National Technical Information Service, 1972), 3: 245-56. The choice of supertanker size and berth number was based upon tankship construction trends and the relative concentration of Gulf and East Coast petroleum refining capacity.

2. For a complete discussion of market prices see M. A. Adelman, The World Petroleum Market (Baltimore: Johns Hopkins University Press, 1972), Chapters 7-8.

3. Ibid., Chapter 7. These independent companies had access to crude oil in the Middle East and were more aggressive about price cutting than the major oil companies.

4. Ibid. By 1972 a barrel of oil in Europe was priced at $10.40, of which $5.60 went to taxes paid to home governments and $1.75 in taxes paid to producers. From the late 1950s to 1970 producing nations were getting less than $1.00 per barrel. The European tax example is provided by Geoffrey Chandler, "The Changing Shape of the Oil Industry," The Petroleum Review (June 1974).

5. The Oil Import Program may be considered a form of tax since the beneficiaries, the oil companies, were able to pocket the difference between foreign and domestic prices. Actually, the license worked more like a tariff than a tax, and before the oil-exporting nations raised their prices there was a substantial debate about changing the program from a license to a tariff. Most economists thought that a tariff was a more equitable and efficient system. The major policy debate is in the Cabinet Task Force on Oil Import Control, The Oil Import Question (Washington, D.C.: U.S. Government Printing Office, 1970). Since 1959, the Oil Import Program has been amended by presidential proclamation until President Ford attempted a gradual $3.00 tariff on foreign oil, which was rescinded. The American consumer paid over 5 billion dollars a year to the industry since the program's inception. The nation only gradually became dependent on foreign oil as a result. Other sources include Robert Baldwin, Nontariff Distortions of International Trade (Washington, D.C.: Brookings, 1970); Senate Interior and Insular Affairs,

Toward a Rational Policy of Oil and Gas Imports, Committee Print, 93rd Congress, Serial 93-94, 1973; and U.S. Congress, Oil and Gas Import Issues, Parts I-III, Hearings before Senate Committee on Interior and Insular Affairs, 1972.

6. U.S. Congress, Senate Committee on Interior and Insular Affairs, U.S. Energy Resources: A Review as of 1972, M. K. Hubbert, Serial 93-40 (Washington, D.C., June 1974). National Academy of Sciences, Mineral Resources and the Environment (Washington, D.C., February 1975).

7. National Petroleum Council, U.S. Energy Outlook (Washington, D.C., December 1972), Chapter 3.

8. Comments by Donald C. Burnham, Energy Policy Project of the Ford Foundation, A Time to Choose (Cambridge, Mass.: Ballinger, 1974), p. 367.

9. Robert R. Nathan Associates, op. cit., Vol. 2, Appendix, Review of Studies of Petroleum Demand and Supply, pp. 99-108.

10. Edward R. Fried and Charles L. Schultz, eds., Higher Prices and the World Economy (Washington, D.C.: Brookings, 1975).

11. Taken from Phillip K. Verlager and Dennis Sheehan, Data Resources, Inc., A Study of the Quarterly Demand for Gasoline and Impacts of Alternative Gasoline Taxes (Lexington, Mass., December 1973), p. III.3. See also H. S. Houthakker and Lester D. Taylor, Consumer Demand in the United States (Cambridge, Mass.: Harvard University Press, 1965).

12. Ford Foundation, A Time to Choose, Table F-2, p. 498.

13. Verlager and Sheehan, Data Resources, Inc., op. cit., p. III.2; Houthakker and Taylor, op. cit., p. 116.

14. National Petroleum Council, U.S. Energy Outlook.

3

THE MOVEMENT OF
PETROLEUM AND TANKSHIP
TRENDS

The need for deepwater ports became apparent as oil tankers of greater size were being built in the shipyards. Increased ocean-borne oil volume and larger carriers made it possible to save considerable sums in the transport of oil. The closing of the Suez Canal demonstrated that tankships too large to use the canal could go around the Cape of Good Hope and still deliver the oil at lower costs.

The savings in delivery costs of oil can be seen in light of unit cost savings, as for instance in cents per barrel for a standard trip. Another approach is to compare the delivery capability of different tanker size classes. By either method of comparison large tankers can be leased for a short or long term at a price that reduces both the unit cost of delivery and delivers more oil per trip. The unit price saving is a result of the economies of construction and operation of larger tankships. The volume of oil delivered per trip is a result of larger size, comparable speeds, and comparable in-port turnaround time.

If it were possible to construct and operate a tanker that is comparable in all respects to other tankers except that it is two to five times the size of older tankers, then size alone is a reasonable index of transport savings.

Larger tankers are wider, longer, and have a deeper draft. It is primarily the vessel draft that represents the physical limitation on existing ports—although length, stopping distance, and turning restrictions are important. The deepest ports on the Gulf and East Coasts are nowhere deep enough to accommodate the larger tankships. This inability to accommodate a fully loaded tankship would persist even if ship design could be altered somewhat to develop a shallow draft fleet.

The economic incentive for deepwater ports is lower unit cost and increased worldwide demand for petroleum. The physical incentive is the insufficient depth of existing ports in the United States.

The relationship between tankship size (measured in deadweight tons), tanker draft, and the water depth of existing U.S. ports is illustrated in Table 3.1. Increasing size and increasing draft are closely correlated. East and Gulf Coast ports accommodate ships up to 80,000 dwt, and only Long Beach on the West Coast can accommodate larger ships. In terms of oil import demand, the East Coast is an area of concentration of consumer demand and the Gulf Coast has the greatest concentration of refineries.

If the principle were followed that a commodity should be delivered as close to its market as possible, then New York/New Jersey and Philadelphia (Delaware Bay) would be the best candidates for a deepwater port.[1] Both ports have considerable refining capacity that could be served by a deepwater terminal. On the Gulf Coast in Texas and in Louisiana even more refinery capacity exists in a concentrated area than any East Coast locations; the East Coast market could also be served by product pipeline or oceangoing barge from the Gulf Coast.

After World War II the typical tankship was a 16,765 deadweight ton vessel (the T-2). The size of tankships has increased rapidly since then with no sacrifice of speed. As shown in Table 3.2, the size characteristics of the world tankship fleet have changed dramatically since the era of the T-2, and since the early 1960s. The last column in Table 3.2 measures the equivalent carrying capacity of increasing size vessels. Comparing size with U.S. port characteristics would indicate that U.S. ports were adequate in the early 1960s, but have ceased to be adequate for the average tankship today. From the two tables it can be inferred that most of the tankships built since 1962 are too large for U.S. ports. The relationship between size and draft is apparent in Table 3.3, where the worldwide construction of ships for private use for 1970 is examined. Generally, there is some variation in the size and draft relationship but the design variation is usually no more than 10 feet of draft for the largest ships of 250,000 dwt.[2]

Although one ship larger than 280,000 dwt was built in 1970, 19 more ships up to 380,000 dwt were delivered by 1972. By 1975 tankers built during the year included 35 vessels over 250,000 dwt, of which 3 were larger than 400,000 dwt. Tankships up to 500,000 dwt are now within range, and there is yet no determination of where diseconomies of size begin to be apparent. There is some opinion that 500,000 dwt is the economic maximum size, but larger ships could be designed up to 1 million dwt.[3]

TABLE 3.1

East Coast Petroleum Ports and Ship Size

Port of Import[a]	Typical Port of Export	Optimum Ship Size[b] (based on distance in thousands dwt)	Draft of Optimum Ship[c] (in feet)	Draft of Port[d] (port of entry in feet)	Permissible Existing Ship Size (in thousands dwt)
Philadelphia	Persian Gulf (via Cape)	280–350	70+	40	80 (Lightered)
New York	Persian Gulf via Suez	220–270	62–70	40	80 (Lightered)
Boston	Caribbean	90–130	46–54	40	60
Chesapeake Bay	West Africa	140–190	54–60	42	60
Hampton Roads	North Africa	140–190	54–60	45	80
Baltimore	Western Europe	90–190	46–60	42	60

[a]Ranked by level of imports of crude oil and products, with Philadelphia, New York, and Boston with approximately 87 percent of the market in 1970 (SOROS Associates).

[b]Based on round-trip distance between ports considering numerable constraints (SOROS Associates).

[c]Sun Oil Company, Philadelphia.

[d]SOROS Associates.

Sources: SOROS Associates, Offshore Terminal System Concepts I (New York, 1972), Chapters 2, 4, and Table 1–20; Sun Oil Company, Analysis of World Tank Ship Fleet: 1970 (Philadelphia, 1971), Figure 2.

TABLE 3.2

World Tankship Fleet

Dec. 31	Number of Vessels	Deadweight Tonnage (thousands)	T-2 Equivalents
1960	3,264	65,780	4,076
1961	3,250	68,859	4,305
1962	3,259	71,996	4,543
1963	3,279	76,179	4,841
1964	3,359	85,126	5,455
1965	3,436	93,172	5,984
1966	3,524	102,909	6,641
1967	3,613	112,366	7,275
1968	3,775	128,128	8,312
1969	3,893	146,029	9,461
1970	3,994	166,774	10,848

Source: Sun Oil Company, Analysis of World Tank Ship Fleet: 1970 (Philadelphia, 1971).

The physical limitation to size is of less importance than market forces in the determination of future size of tankships. Larger ships have been constructed rapidly in the recent past, partly as a result of competition. Now there is considerable evidence that in this highly competitive business tankship overcapacity, already present in the 1975 market, will continue to 1980. Large ships would still tend to capture the market from small ships for the long haul, but the overall world price would drop.* Lower profits may squeeze out the small or overcapitalized shipowner. Moreover, the older and smaller ships may be retired sooner.

The average age of the world tankship fleet has declined since 1967 from seven years and nine months to seven years and one month. Although this decline has not been great, it has been downward or steady since 1967. Noel Mostert reports that the write-off

---

*Although there is competition in the sense that the larger, newer, and more efficient ships can command the market, the routes over which such ships compete are limited. As a result every size ship may have a market niche for which it is best suited.

life of a supertanker is ten years, which is some indication that economy takes precedence over other considerations, particularly in this highly competitive market.

TABLE 3.3

Drafts of Oil Tankers Built During 1970

Mdwt Class*	Number of Ships	Average Dwt	Average Draft (ft.)
20- 29	13	26,832	34.7
60- 69	2	61,792	43.2
70- 79	4	76,433	42.2
80- 89	3	82,794	44.3
90- 99	5	97,154	47.4
100-109	3	101,946	48.2
110-119	3	112,663	51.6
120-129	2	125,210	52.2
130-139	4	136,058	54.8
140-149	3	143,270	55.0
160-169	2	161,935	64.5
190-199	1	192,320	58.6
200-209	12	204,595	62.3
210-219	30	215,157	63.5
220-229	11	225,432	65.5
230-239	1	233,000	67.0
240-249	5	248,496	65.8
250-259	8	251,692	65.7
280-289	1	280,420	71.4
Total	113	168,638 (average)	

*Mdwt are million deadweight tons.

Note: Excludes government-owned tankers, O/O, B/O, O/B/O, and specialty carriers. O/O refers to ore/oil and O/B/O is ore/bulk/oil carrier.

Sources: The Tanker Register (London: H. Clarkson and Co. Ltd., 1971); Sun Oil Company, Analysis of World Tank Ship Fleet: 1970 (Philadelphia, 1971).

One example of the rapid expansion of fleets is the increase in size of the Japanese fleet. Japan leads all other countries in ship construction, and builds more ships for export than any other country. In four years (1969-72), Japan had more than doubled the size of her fleet. The average age of her fleet is just four years (which is a little less than the length of time the average American keeps his automobile). Such expansion would be expected to be fostered by a nation so heavily dependent upon maritime commerce and raw material imports. Nevertheless, tankship size and deepwater port development are not isolated phenomena, and are apparent in both oil-producing countries and in Europe.

Although ships are getting larger (Table 3.4), the wide disparity in fleet size by country is both an index of the age of a nation's fleet and the status of deepwater ports. Europe and Japan lead in orders on tankship size that represent their import needs and their ability to accommodate such ships at their ports. Although the worldwide demand for oil has fallen off with the increase in price, the existing overcapacity in fleet would not diminish the long-run advantages of large tankships.

A comparison of Table 3.1 and Table 3.5 indicates the differing position of the United States and the rest of the world. In the United States there is no port that is capable of handling ships of larger size than 80,000 dwt. Even a ship of this size would require lightering--a practice that has certain oil spill risks.[4] Comparing typical U.S. receiving ports with typical delivery port areas would indicate long journeys for either refined or crude oil. A judgmental evaluation of optimum vessel size shows that even a relatively short trip from the Caribbean calls for a larger ship than East Coast ports can accommodate. Worldwide there are many ports that can handle vessels of more than 150,000 dwt (Table 3.5). These ports represent both importing and exporting areas. The Persian Gulf, North Africa, Venezuela, and Nigeria represent leading areas of export. Europe, the British Isles, and Japan are leading areas of import. When oil is imported to the East Coast several ports may be used as transshipment terminals. In the Bahamas, Freeport may be used for long journeys and in Canada, Saint John, Port Tupper, and Come-By-Chance may be used. These transshipment ports would be points at which smaller vessels could pick up oil destined for the East Coast. As a general rule, this transshipment alternative is less attractive than a deepwater port much closer to refineries near the center of market demand. There are circumstances, such as the high cost of dredging existing ports, that make transshipment attractive.

TABLE 3.4

The Growth of the World Tanker and Combination Carrier Fleets, 1969-74

(in thousands dwt)

	January 1969	January 1970	January 1971	January 1972	January 1973	January 1974
Tankers						
10,000-30,000 dwt	29,930	29,204	29,018	29,251	28,304	28,164
30,000-175,000 dwt	78,722	83,275	87,327	90,185	92,379	95,812
Over 175,000 dwt	5,465	17,102	32,880	49,379	66,564	89,324
Total	114,117	129,581	149,225	168,815	187,247	213,300
Combination carriers						
Ore/oil carriers	5,899	7,047	8,557	11,017	15,811	20,809
Ore/bulk/oil carriers	4,295	5,151	6,781	9,753	12,723	16,017
Total	10,194	12,198	15,338	20,770	28,534	36,826

Sources: Tankers: John J. Jacobs and Co., Ltd.; combination carriers: Fearnley and Eger's Chartering Co., Ltd.; Organization for Economic Cooperation and Development, Maritime Transport 1973 (Paris, 1974), pp. 20, 56.

TABLE 3.5

Representative Crude Oil Ports
(capable of accommodating 150,000 dwt vessels)

Japan*	Persian Gulf
Niigotata	Ras Al Khafji, Saudi Arabia
Tokyo Bay	Ras Tanura, Saudi Arabia
Kiire	Das Island, Trucial States
Yokkaichi	Mina Al Ahmadi, Kuwait
North and West Africa	Kharg Island, Iran
Marsa El Brega, Libya	Western Hemisphere
Forcados, Nigeria	Puerto La Cruz, Venezuela
Port Said, Egypt	Freeport, Bahamas
Southern Europe	Saint John, Canada
Algeciras, Spain	Port Tupper, Canada
Bilbao, Spain	Come-By-Chance, Canada
Marseilles (La Fos), France	Northern Europe
Trieste, Yugoslavia	Le Havre, France
England, Scotland, and Ireland	Dunkirk, France
Foulness, England	Rotterdam, Netherlands
Liverpool, England	Goteburg, Sweden
Glasgow, Scotland	Helgoland, Germany
Milford Haven, England	Hamburg, Germany
Bantry Bay, Ireland	

*Japanese ports include at least 16 deepwater berths.
Sources: Arthur D. Little, Foreign Deepwater Port Develop-
ments, 3 vols. (Springfield, Va.: National Technical Information
Service, 1971), 3:6–40, Table G-7; SOROS Associates, Offshore
Terminal System Concepts I (New York, 1972), Figure 1-38.

Import trends and size of market considerations have provided
the impetus to tankship construction. The increase in worldwide
movement of oil in the last few years has been a significant factor
also. As well, the length of an average trip has increased as Japan
and the United States have become important import areas relative
to Europe. Another factor is the closing of the Suez Canal, whose
reopening is likely to reduce the ton-mile volume of crude oil movement by 10 percent.[5] As length of haul increases, the market for
large tankships grows. As the United States becomes an important
import area, another long-haul market for tankships is available.

Recent annual increases in tonnage shipments worldwide have been between 4 percent and 13 percent since 1965-66 (Table 3. 6). Ton miles of transportation have increased at a faster rate--between 7 and 16 percent. The latter index is more pertinent to large tank-ship construction trends, because of an increase in long-haul markets. By any measure of trade growth these increases would prompt expansion in supply capability and would provide a good freight market for shipowners.

TABLE 3.6

International Seaborne Trade in Crude
Oil and Petroleum Products

Period	Tonnage Shipments	Ton-Mile Transport Performance
	(percent increase per annum)	
1965-66	10	7
1966-67	8	24
1967-68	13	20
1968-69	11	13
1969-70	15	16
1970-71	6	15
1971-72	10	16
1972-73	13	18
1973-74	-1	-4
1974-75 (est.)	-11	-9

Source: Fearnley and Egers Chartering Co., Ltd., Review 1975 (Oslo, Norway, January 1976), p. 14.

Consistent with the growth in petroleum movement, world tankship construction has increased both in vessel size and total fleet. The size distribution (Table 3.4) shows how the smallest size vessel, 10,000 to 30,000 dwt, has remained constant in total deadweight tons, but the largest class total tonnage has increased tremendously. Combination carriers have also increased, allowing for additional flexibility. Combination carriers can carry cargoes other than oil rather than return to the export port in ballast. In addition to being able to use a triangular route (for example, oil from Persian Gulf to Hampton Roads, Virginia, and coal to Japan),

combination carriers can compete in different raw-material markets
depending on charter prices.

A longer period comparison (Tables 3.7 and 3.8) shows that
worldwide oil imports have been increasing at more than 9 percent
annually (1950-72) and the increase has been reasonably stable in
the four five-year periods since 1950. Tankship construction has increased 8.6 percent from 1950 to 1973. The similarity in tankship
construction and oil-market volume trends (about 9 percent per year)
shows a close correlation between the supply and demand for oil
transport. Only very recently have tankship construction and ship-
yard orders increased more rapidly than the outlook for oil sea trade.
The present market is bleak with no growth in petroleum consumption
in two years. As tankships are built, the supply continues to outstrip
demand, unlike the approximate balance achieved in former years.[6]

TABLE 3.7

Ocean Commodity Movement--Type of Cargo

Period	Average Annual Percentage Increase		
	Dry Cargo	Oil	Total
1950-72	6.5	9.4	7.9
1950-55	8.5	9.3	8.7
1955-60	3.8	9.0	6.2
1960-65	7.6	9.7	8.6
1965-70	7.3	10.5	9.0
1970-71	1.0	7.0	4.0
1971-72	6.0	7.0	7.0

Sources: United Nations, Monthly Bulletin of Statistics; Organization for Economic Cooperation and Development, Maritime
Transport 1973 (Paris, 1974), pp. 23, 47.

In 1970 the United States had begun to import a large volume
of oil, and between 1970 and 1973 imported oil increased from 23 to
36 percent of the U.S. total petroleum market. Relative to oil flow
from the Persian Gulf to Europe or Japan, the U.S. market was not
important in 1970. By 1972 North American oil imports were a little
over 7 percent of total bulk commodity shipping demand. In contrast,
Japanese oil imports were nearly 12 percent and European imports
were more than 37 percent. Both Japan and Europe represent more

concentrated markets, where a few ports could handle the distribution to the hinterland. The importance of petroleum to Europe and Japan is shown in Table 3.9, where oil volume is considered relative to the main bulk commodity movements (oil, iron ore, and coal). If these three commodities represent about 85 percent of all bulk movement, then oil to Europe and Japan makes up more than 60 percent of these three. Oil is the leading bulk commodity in trade and nearly all of the imports are in Europe and Japan. Representing geographically small areas, a high-capacity vessel such as a supertanker is a logical method of transport. The Middle East exports about 70 percent of all worldwide oil. As the figure depicts, this concentration of movement provides considerable opportunity for large carriers.

TABLE 3.8

Ocean Commodity Movement--Type of Vessel

Period (mid-year/mid-year)[b]	Average Annual Increase (in terms of grt)[a]		
	Nontankers	Tankers	Total
1950-73	4.3	8.6	5.6
1950-55	1.8	9.2	3.5
1955-60	3.7	9.3	5.4
1960-65	3.8	5.9	4.5
1965-70	6.2	9.4	7.4
1970-71	6.9	11.6	8.7
1971-72	8.2	9.4	8.7
1972-73	7.1	9.7	8.1
1973-74[b]	3.5	3.1	3.4
1974-75[b]	3.6	3.4	3.6

[a]Gross registered tons.

[b]Estimate based upon dwt rather than grt. Combined carriers are put in the nontanker category for 1973-75. Also 1973-75 estimates are first of year to first of year rather than mid-year changes.

Note: These figures exclude the Canadian and U.S. Great Lakes fleets. If this tonnage is included the figures are: mid-1972: 268.3 million grt, increase 1971-72: 8.6 percent; mid-1973: 289.9 million grt, increase 1972-73: 8.0 percent.

Sources: Lloyd's Register of Shipping; Organization for Economic Cooperation and Development, Maritime Transport 1973 (Paris, 1974), pp. 23, 47; Fearnley and Egers Chartering Co. Ltd., Review 1975 (Oslo, Norway, January 1976), p. 15.

TABLE 3.9

The Importance for World Shipping of the Main Regional Bulk Commodity Imports, 1972

	Japan	Western Europe	North America	Main OECD Regions	All Others	Total Oil/Ore/Coal
Oil Imports						
Percent of total oil/ore/ coal shipping demand*	14.8	46.8	9.0	70.6	14.1	84.7
Percent of total shipping demand*	11.8	37.4	7.2	56.4	11.2	67.6
Iron ore imports						
Percent of total oil/ore coal shipping demand*	6.5	2.8	0.7	10.0	1.1	11.1
Percent of total shipping demand*	5.2	2.2	0.5	7.9	0.9	8.8
Coal imports						
Percent of total oil/ore/ coal shipping demand*	2.9	1.2	--	4.1	0.1	4.2
Percent of total shipping demand*	2.3	1.0	--	3.3	0.1	3.4
Total oil/ore/coal imports						
Percent of total oil/ore/ coal shipping demand*	24.2	50.8	9.7	84.7	15.3	100.0
Percent of total shipping demand*	19.3	40.6	7.7	67.6	12.2	79.8

*Measured in ton-miles.

Sources: Derived mainly from Fearnley and Eger's Chartering Co. Ltd. and BP Trading Co.; Organization for Economic Cooperation and Development (OECD), Maritime Transport 1973 (Paris, 1974), p. 25.

In one sense the United States represents an addition to this
worldwide commerce. Oil imports to the United States doubled between 1967-73. During this short period of time, deepwater ports
were under construction throughout the world. As U.S. imports
grow it is logical that East and Gulf Coasts are added to the worldwide network of deepwater ports. It is also true that in a slow-
growth consumption period, domestic refiners prefer to import
crude oil rather than products as they have the additional capacity.
Such a preference was evident in 1975.

Often these ports are terminals rather than a large port city
handling all kinds of commodities, where bulk imports are used in
manufacturing or further processed within the port district. As
noted in Table 3.5, the many deepwater ports would not be familiar
names to most people. Rotterdam is well known, but Kharg Island
or Bantry Bay are hardly port cities. Many of these latter ports
are terminals where transshipment occurs. In the case of a loading
port, the terminal may be linked to the oil fields directly. At receiving terminals the oil may be passed on overland by pipeline or
transshipped by sea. The terminals may be constructed on islands,
in natural harbors, or at sea. The berthing facilities may be fixed
similar to the usual docking arrangements or the ship may be "tied"
to a fixed buoy. In the latter case, the vessel is free to rotate with
wind and wave action. The latter arrangement is less expensive,
and is less protective from heavy seas when the berthing facility is
offshore rather than in natural bays and harbors. These terminals,
often located far from urban centers, may or may not be convenient
locations for refineries. Where a terminal is on a "sea island" or
uses the buoy concept, popular in petroleum company advertisements,
there may be neither adequate land nor a convenient market center
for such refining activity. In the case of a monobuoy or multibuoy
terminal, the terminal may be linked by pipeline (or barge) to onshore refineries. Regardless of how a terminal may be linked to
refinery centers, each terminal has storage capacity nearby. Large
tankships many days at sea arrive in not wholly predictable patterns.
As the vessels discharge their oil, some oil must be stored in large
tanks near the terminal. In periods of closely timed ship arrivals,
the oil is stored and during periods of few ship arrivals, the oil is
drawn from the tanks into other smaller tankers, coastal barges, or
through pipelines.

A deepwater port may be a well-known port city blessed with
a naturally deep harbor or dredged to accommodate large tankships.
The port may be close to the original city, but owing to the cost of
dredging and lack of space, the terminal facilities have moved to the
mouth of the harbor. London, Philadelphia, and many other port
cities have remained ports in this manner. A deepwater port may

also be a terminal with the essentials of docking facilities and storage tanks--where ships leave nowhere and arrive nowhere, far from human pursuits. The only distinguishable features of a deepwater port are the draft of the harbor, the turning basin, and the width and length of maneuvering areas.

COST ECONOMIES OF LARGE TANKSHIPS

There are several ways of looking at economy. One way is to compare the transport cost per barrel in large tankships to the cost of carriage in smaller ships. Earlier it was pointed out that for the Persian Gulf trade to the East or Gulf Coast size alone may be a reasonable index of economy. Another approach is to merely calculate the estimated savings that may be expected from using larger ships. By way of illustration, the Department of Commerce showed that in 1969 a 200,000 dwt tankship from Kuwait to North America could deliver oil at 40 cents per barrel, but a 50,000 dwt vessel would deliver oil for 89 cents per barrel. This savings of 49 cents would be less if the 200,000 dwt vessel were compared to a 100,000 dwt ship as shown in Table 3.10. The Draft Environmental Impact Statement on deepwater ports made comparisons that indicated savings of 33 cents per barrel (265,000 dwt compared to 65,000 dwt).[7]

TABLE 3.10

Economics of Deepwater Distribution Terminals

Voyage	Distance in Miles	Cost/Barrel Size of Tanker x 1,000 dwt				
		500	300	200	100	50
Kuwait-Mediterranean via Cape of Good Hope	11,086	.242	.305	.374	.576	.835
Kuwait-North America via Cape of Good Hope	11,856	.259	.326	.400	.616	.894
Kuwait-Japan	6,615	.160	.202	.248	.381	.552
Distribution	500	--	--	--	.064	.079

Sources: W. S. McPhee, Crude Oil Transshipment Terminals, presented at Society of Marine Port Engineers (Fort Schuyler, New York, March 1969); U.S. Department of Commerce, The Economics of Deepwater Terminals (Washington, D.C.: U.S. Government Printing Office, 1972), p. 8.

Cent-per-barrel comparisons are not strictly due to the economies of large tankships, but reflect the tankship market. For example, a later evaluation of deepwater ports for Louisiana used an
estimated savings of 19 cents per barrel.[8] Large tankers will save
money over existing alternatives, and the actual per unit savings will
depend upon the market over the period of the investment. As a result, the profits to the terminal operator depend upon his capital cost,
the market, and the volume of petroleum the terminal will serve.

The tankship market, as with any competitive market, can be
quite intricate in its day-to-day operation. Major analyses on the
subject describe long- and short-term arrangements available to
tanker charterers and tanker owners.[9] Short-run considerations
are governed by immediate availability of tankers and long-run considerations, when all costs are variable, depend upon the cost of
ship building, and the long-run expected market price. This cost
of building and operating ships impacts the shorter "term" rates and
even has some impact on the "voyage" or "spot" ship hire.[10] In
gauging costs and long-term rates, it is important to know what type
of ship the market will absorb at what price since one is gauging a
future market. M. A. Adelman estimates that by 1979 the average
annual tankship rate may decline from world-scale 110 to world-
scale 43, representing a decline in the Persian Gulf to Europe shipping cost of $1.30 to $0.50 per barrel. World scale is merely a
price index. A long-term rate of world-scale 40 may be likely with
an incremental ship of a type that is over 250,000 dwt.[11] This discussion of long-term rates is in the context of future rates in a market that fluctuates considerably.

TANKSHIP MARKET 1973-75

During 1973 tankships were in great demand and the market
was up. "The rate for five-year charters of VLCCs that had equated
through 1972 to between world-scale 52 and world-scale 58 had risen
by October 1973 to just under world-scale 100. Then after the crisis,
demand slackened and rates started to fall until by February 1974,
they were below world-scale 90."[12] Rates fell because OPEC had cut
production and raised prices. The cost of operating a tankship increased, however, because bunker prices rose from $20 per ton to
$70 per ton.[13] Throughout 1974 the market declined for all ships
and particularly for the long-haul crude market. From January 1974
to December 1974 the market declined fairly steadily. An example
is the Persian Gulf-United Kingdom route via the Cape. World-
scale decline was from about 95 to 40 by December of 1974. Actually, rates were much lower than the world-scale index showed, as the

index was not adjusted for the use of bunker prices.[14] With the index adjusted, world scale for this route declined to 25 and 30. These
rates are below total costs for tankships and do not cover all variable
tankship costs.

Tracking the Persian Gulf-U.K. route via the Cape reveals that
several 200,000 dwt vessels and larger ships took world-scale 17.5
in January and March of 1975.[15] Several VLCC vessels took a world-
scale 15 through April and May. In August, the VLCC was back to
the world-scale 20-30 range. H. P. Dewry calculates that a 250,000
dwt vessel needs a world-scale rate of 21 to cover voyage costs (marginal costs) and by slow steaming can get by with a world-scale 16.
Depressed 1975 prices meant that these vessels were not covering
all their variable costs, which include crew, insurance, and the like.
The voyage costs (marginal costs) together with the operation costs
make up the variable costs, which require a world scale of 28, even
with slow steaming.[16] The costs of a single voyage, such as bunkers,
can be distinguished from other operating costs and hull costs--the
latter representing fixed costs of investment. In the long run the
250,000 dwt vessel would require a world scale of 72 in order to pay
off debt, operate the tanker at optimum speed, and earn a 15 percent
return on investment.

In such a depressed market as 1974-75, it takes some reserves
to stay in business, and many ships are being laid up and an increasing number are being scrapped.

In the depressed markets of 1974 and 1975, tankship owners are
forced to take charters at prices that reflect their costs. Often, the
dilemma is whether to take a charter that just covers the cost of a
voyage, whether to "lay up" the ship and wait for better times (reduce operating costs such as insurance), or whether to scrap or sell
the vessel.

Such a depressed market reduces the advantages of a deepwater port. Shipping prices are so low due to overcapacity that differences in how the petroleum is carried are less important. As
noted in the next section, the advantages of deepwater ports become
less apparent in such a market. Nevertheless, it cannot be assumed
that tankship overcapacity will exist indefinitely. The more permanent advantages of a deepwater port must be based on a long-term
market, where the peaks and troughs of the market (1973-75 for example) are not used as a basis for comparison.

TANKSHIP SIZE/PRICE DIFFERENTIAL

Rather than follow these fluctuations of the market, the oil
terminal decision focuses on the more permanent differences between

alternative transportation systems. Two data are useful: the difference between one size carrier and another over time, and the long-term outlook for different vessel classes.

Using the monthly average freight rate assessment (AFRA) tanker rate, which is another price index, certain trends can be examined (Table 3.11). Comparing two sizes of tankships--45,000 to 79,999 and 80,000 to 159,999 dwt--the spread between size/class freight price can be shown. Larger ships are an advantage for long-haul routes and many middle-distance routes of 3,000 to 6,000 miles. Average savings of 17 cents per barrel are shown for the Persian Gulf to U.S. route. Greater savings would be indicated if a typical vessel in the lower range were compared to vessels of 200,000 dwt or larger. The size/price disparity appears rather constant despite the greater fluctuation in overall price. For example, the price for the 80,000 to 159,000 dwt size tanker doubled during 1973, but the spread between this price and the price for the next lower class remained fairly constant. The inference is that whether the market is good or bad, larger tankers will have a consistent advantage over the smaller vessels.

TABLE 3.11

Average Difference in Cost per Barrel
for Two Tanker Size Classes (1970-72)[a]
(in cents)

Route	1970[b]	1971[b]	1972[c]	1973[c]
U.S. Gulf to New York	3	4	3	3
Ras Tanura to New York				
(via Cape)	16	17	16	14
Sidon, Lebanon to New York	7	8	7	7
Ras Tanura to United Kingdom				
(via Cape)	15	17	16	--
Ras Tanura to Rotterdam				
(via Cape)	--	--	14	15

[a]Difference in monthly price between 45,000-79,000 dwt vessels compared to 80,000-160,000 dwt vessels in U.S. dollars per barrel of 34-degree gravity crude from Platt's Oilgram 1973 edition.

[b]Data for 1970-71 based on two months.

[c]Data for 1972-73 based on 12 months, except Ras Tanura to United Kingdom (four months) and Ras Tanura to Rotterdam (eight months).

Source: Platt's Oilgram Price Service, Platt's Oilgram (New York: McGraw-Hill, 1973).

For 1974 it is possible to compare these differences in terms
of world-scale VLCC class (160,000 to 320,000 dwt) compared to the
large carrier "2" class (80,000 to 160,000 dwt). From January
1974 to October 1974, the AFRA monthly index in world scale showed
that the advantage of the VLCC declined from 20.5 points to 13.2
points.[17] Assuming world scale at 100 is equivalent to $1.40 barrel;
this difference is valued at 18 cents per barrel at the low range in
October and 28 cents per barrel at the high range in January 1974.

TANKSHIP SIZE/PRICE DIFFERENCE
IN A DEPRESSED MARKET

As noted before, 1975 was a low point for tankship owners.
Looking again at the AFRA monthly index, the VLCC class was estimated at 57.7 through July 15 to August 15, 1975, and the next
lower-size class (large range 2) was estimated at 64.0.[18] With the
world-scale index higher due to the cost of bunkers, the per barrel
cost to transport oil is $1.98. At this world-scale level the differ-
ence between the VLCC and the next lower vessel size is merely
seven cents a barrel.

Clearly, the depressed market tends to reduce the price differences between tankship sizes. The larger vessels do not lose
their advantages entirely, however, as shown in Figure 3.1. The
variable nature of the spot market is noted in the United Kingdom-
Cape route for tankships from January to November of 1975. There
is a tendency, however, as shown in the overall size/price relationship, to have lower prices with larger ships. This tendency is
clearer when different periods are examined separately. Over ten
months the VLCC was chartered for prices ranging from $2.16 per
ton to $5.05 per ton for this particular route. Based upon the data,
215,000 dwt and larger size vessel cargoes showed an average price
per ton of $3.19 for the ten months. The next discrete size, for ex-
ample, 115,000 dwt to 170,000 dwt, showed an average cargo rate of
$3.59 per ton. This difference of 40 cents per ton is about 5 cents
per barrel. Five cents a barrel is very close to the AFRA monthly
rate difference noted for July 15 to August 15 when VLCC is compared to large-range 2 (80,000 dwt to 160,000 dwt).

Despite the narrowing differences between tankships, smaller
vessels will still take a higher price than a VLCC. Higher costs require that the smaller vessels take higher prices even in a depressed
market.

In the long run, the advantage of the deepwater port is comparable to the long-run cost advantage of the most economical long-haul
carrier. W. L. Nelson has calculated this cost as well as the
change in transport prices over time. All of these comparisons are

FIGURE 3.1

Spot Tanker Rates: Persian Gulf to United Kingdom
via Cape Route, January–November 1975
(dollars per ton)

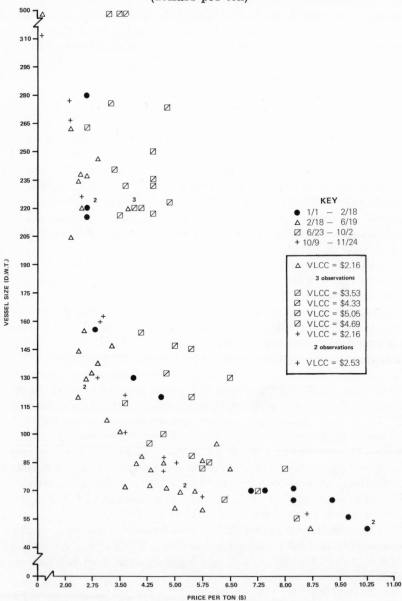

Source: Platt's Oilgram Price Service, *Platt's Oilgram*, 50th ed. (New York: McGraw-Hill, 1975).

in terms of world scale. Owing to the productivity of the larger
ships, the annual price index for transportation in world scale has
been: 89.9 (1960), 72.3 (1962), 90.0 (1964), 67.0 (1966), 74.4 (1968),
82.6 (1970), 68.8 (1972), and 80.0 (1973). During these same years
the average price of a 58,000 dwt vessel has moved slowly upward.
Through 1969 this vessel size was slightly cheaper than the average
oil delivery price, but after 1969 it became more expensive: 87.1
(1970), 77.1 (1972), and 92.4 (1973). The trend toward larger size
has meant that larger, less-expensive supertankers have kept prices
stable throughout the 1960s even though any one sized vessel has
shown slowly increasing and less competitive cost.

Nelson has also calculated the break-even world-scale rate for
different size vessels: 30,000 dwt (61.5), 60,000 (44), 90,000 (37.5),
120,000 (34), 160,000 (31.5), 200,000 (30), 250,000 (28), and 300,000
(27).[19] The per-barrel or per-ton transport cost of the large tankship is much less than the smaller vessels and thereby accounts for
the productivity in petroleum movement. For example, the break-
even world-scale 44 of a 60,000 dwt vessel is 46 percent more expensive than the break-even W 30 of a 200,000 dwt vessel. At a
worldwide average market of 80.0 (1973), both the 60,000 and the
200,000 dwt ships make profits, but with an estimated long-term
rate of world-scale 40, only the larger vessel can make a profit
where the two vessels compete. Nelson's estimates are based on
world-scale rates of 1974 and therefore should be increased about
40 percent.

Nelson's estimates are lower than the 250,000 ton total trading
costs given by H. P. Dewry. As noted earlier, Dewry estimated
that the full costs of a 250,000 dwt vessel was world-scale 72, assuming a 15 percent return on investment.[20] Whatever differences there
are in these estimates, the long-run differential in tankship break-
even cost provides an index to the long-run advantage of deepwater
ports over existing ports.

FUTURE OUTLOOK FOR VLCC AND THE SUEZ CANAL

The long-run outlook for large tankships depends upon the
market for the incremental ship and the break-even cost for various
size ships. For the next few years, until 1980, the existing VLCC
overcapacity is a major determinant of transport prices. Planners
for SEADOCK and LOOP are more concerned about the post-1980
era. Nevertheless, the near-term future provides a guide for the
market when prices are low.

H. P. Dewry has developed an evaluation of likely trends in
bringing vessel availability back into line with the demand for

petroleum movement. In developing the analysis, Dewry makes use of the general opinion that the Suez Canal will have little impact on tankship trends.[21] Under nearly all conditions postulated by the author there will be a tankship surplus in 1977 and 1980. When such surplus prevails, rates are assumed to be low and all trade takes the Cape route. Slow steaming will also be the norm. Only when there is a shortage of tankships is it assumed that smaller vessels will be used on the Suez Canal route. In other words, the Cape route using the VLCC is the least expensive alternative unless there is a shortage of shipping.

The perspective on tankship overcapacity is shared in the industry.[22] The Suez Canal opened with much fanfare, but the judgment is that it will not affect trading very much.[23] By August 1975, two months after reopening, the Canal registered less than 5 percent of its preclosure levels in the oil trade.[24] In September the Canal had less than 10 percent of the volume it carried in September 1966 before closure. Only 41 tankers used the Canal in September 1975.[25] Judging by the tanker spot market of the Persian Gulf-Cape route to the United Kingdom, the reopening of the Canal did not affect prices. VLCCs were obtaining about the same prices after the Canal reopened.

The Canal reopened at a point when the tanker market is at its most depressed condition in years. Although the Canal could do better in the future, it clearly does not have a comparative advantage. If the market turned to a tankship shortage position, the shorter Suez Canal route would be valuable in cutting time and increasing tankship utilization. Such a role, however, makes the Canal a marginal consideration in world tanker trade.

DELIVERY CAPABILITY OF THE VLCC
INDEPENDENT OF MARKET

A transportation planner would look at the real logistic advantages as an index of performance and cost as well as market trends. These logistic advantages are greater when a dedicated system is considered, whereby a petroleum company operates both the sending and receiving terminal. In circumstances where a company can operate terminals, tankships, and refineries it would not be necessary to enter the tankship market. Rather the tankships would be owned and the fleet makeup would depend on a combination of factors related to terminals, demand, and tankship usage. In any case, market trends in tankships would be a peripheral consideration, more important to marginal tankship investment decisions than as a mainstay of oil movement. An alternative to ownership is a long-term lease.

LARGE TANKSHIP DELIVERY CAPABILITY

A method of comparing tankship size is presented in Analysis of World Tank Ships: 1970. Compared were turnaround time, speed, cargo capacity, and fuel consumption. The following assumptions were used:[26]

1. Round-trip bunkers from the loading port
2. Five days of reserve fuel aboard
3. Stores and provisions ranging from 300 tons to 500 tons on 30 mdwt to 325 mdwt tankers
4. 7.45 barrels of oil per long ton as a typical gravity
5. Port time of 1.6 days for loading and 2.0 days for discharging
6. One transit of the Panama Canal takes .75 days while the Suez passage takes 1.0 days
7. The amount of cargo that a vessel can carry during a 347-day operating year was averaged over a 365-day period resulting in the average cargo-delivery capability in barrels per day.

The results in Figure 3.2 point out the advantage of large tankships. This advantage exists for East Coast trade because large ships used on most of a route saves money, even if the oil is transshipped in Canada. If no deepwater port capability exists on the East Coast, then either transshipment must occur or a dedicated fleet of smaller vessels must be retained to serve the market.

A tabular presentation of the analysis, using the same assumptions, shows how oil can be delivered to Port Tupper, Nova Scotia (Table 3.12). Using representative loading ports in Africa and the Persian Gulf, a typical 150,000 dwt vessel can deliver more than twice the oil per day as a 70,000 dwt vessel can. This comparison does not indicate that a delivery would be made every day, only that thousands of barrels of oil in a typical vessel spread over the period of arrivals would average the barrels per day shown in the table. For a 150,000 dwt vessel, the oil delivery capability to Nova Scotia is no less for relatively short trips from Puerto La Cruz, Venezuela, than for longer trips from Africa.

In comparing oil delivery capability to Philadelphia (Table 3.13), only the smaller tankships of 30,000 and 70,000 dwt were evaluated. Since these classes represent the upper limit in draft (Figure 3.3), then the larger tankship sizes are omitted. In terms of delivery capability, transshipment from Port Tupper (for Persian Gulf or African oil bound for Philadelphia) is a viable alternative to direct shipment in 70,000 dwt vessels. These delivery comparisons

FIGURE 3.2

Vessel Performance: Cargo Delivery Capability
Versus Round-Trip Distance

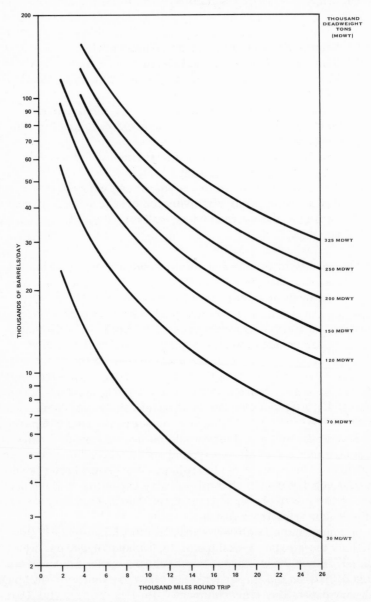

Source: Sun Oil Company, Analysis of World Tankships 1970
(Philadelphia, August 1971).

TABLE 3.12

Average Cargo Delivery Capability to Point Tupper, Nova Scotia
(thousands of barrels per day)

From	Mina Al Ahmadi, Kuwait (Cape)	Mina Al Ahmadi, Kuwait (Cape-Suez)	Mina Al Ahmadi, Kuwait (Suez)	Sidon, Lebanon	Escravos, Nigeria	Es Sider, Libya	Puerto La Cruz, Venezuela
R.T. Miles	23,160	19,391	15,622	9,410	9,062	8,088	4,268
Mdwt							
30	2.8	--	4.1	7.2	7.4	8.2	14.1
70	7.3	--	10.4	17.6	18.2	20.2	34.2
120	12.7	14.8	--	29.9	30.9	34.1	57.7
150	16.1	18.8	--	37.7	39.0	43.1	72.6
200	21.2	24.7	--	--	51.1	56.5	--
250	26.8	--	--	--	64.4	--	--
325	34.1	--	--	--	--	--	--

Source: Sun Oil Company, Analysis of World Tank Ships 1970 (Philadelphia, August 1971).

apply to transshipment of Caribbean oil bound for the East Coast and the Gulf Coast, as well as they do to Canadian transshipment. The figures indicate that a combination of supertanker and smaller vessel can be used to reduce transport cost without an East Coast port. This option exists so long as an adequate transshipment terminal is available to accommodate the VLCC.

TABLE 3.13

Average Cargo Delivery Capability to Philadelphia
(thousands of barrels per day)

From	R. T. Miles	Mdwt	
		30	70
Mina Al Ahmadi, Kuwait (Cape)	23,956	2.7	7.1
Mina Al Ahmadi, Kuwait (Suez)	16,922	3.8	9.6
Sidon, Lebanon	10,710	6.3	15.7
Escravos, Nigeria	10,128	6.7	16.5
Es Sider, Libya	9,388	7.2	17.7
Puerto La Cruz, Venezuela	3,800	15.5	37.3
Galveston, Texas	3,696	15.8	38.0
Point Tupper, Nova Scotia	1,810	25.2	60.3

Source: Sun Oil Company, Analysis of World Tank Ships 1970 (Philadelphia, August 1971).

Although illustrative, transshipment has proven profitable. In a petroleum world where market trends fluctuate, both for the price of oil and in the supply/demand clearing price of the transport market, then a number of "next best" solutions must be considered. For example, the price of oil to the consumer or the distributor may depend on taxes of all kinds, rather than transport costs. Tax advantages in siting terminals, or the price deliberations of the OPEC cartel weigh far more heavily on investment decisions than do transport-network optimizations.[27] These industry uncertainties do not diminish the principle that large tankship delivery near the center of market is advantageous. But relative to a quadrupled price per barrel, transport is less significant to the oil companies than it was a few years ago. Money can still be made and saved but ranked on a list of priorities, transport is lower than it was when crude oil was $3.00 a barrel.

FIGURE 3.3

Draft Versus Deadweight
(60 mdwt to 250 mdwt tankers)

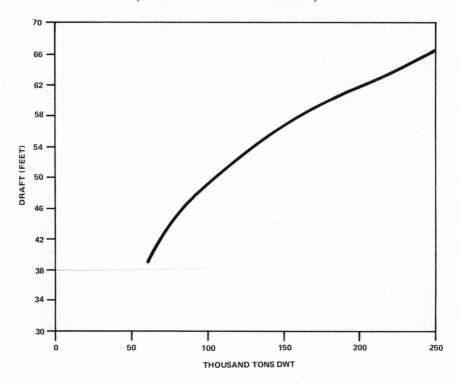

TANK SHIPS		DISCHARGE PORT DEPTH LIMITATION — FT.
DWT CLASS	DRAFT FT.	
30,000	34.6	35 Ft. — New York and New Jersey Channels
50,000	39.5	40 Ft. — Philadelphia, Pa. to Sea
70,000	41.9	40 Ft. — Mississippi River to Gulf
120,000	51.9	40 Ft. — Houston Ship Channel
150,000	54.2	54 Ft. — Long Beach, Calif.
200,000	61.8	
250,000	65.5	
325,000	81.4	

Source: Sun Oil Company, Analysis of World Tankships 1970 (Philadelphia, August 1971).

73

TABLE 3.14

Cost of Tanker Alternatives

(from Kuwait to Milford Haven and Rotterdam)

Tanker Size (dwt)	At	Direct 80,000		Direct 225,000		Transshipment 326,000 to Bantry Bay / 80,000 to Milford/Rotterdam	
		Low	High	Low	High	Low	High
Comparable worldscale (percent)	100	74	93	56	66	48 + 74	62 + 93
Kuwait to Milford Haven	$8.90	$6.59	$8.28	$4.98	$5.88	--	--
Milford Haven transshipped at Bantry Bay	$8.74 + .78	--	--	--	--	$4.28 + 0.58	$5.41 + 0.72
Kuwait to Rotterdam	$9.17	$6.79	$8.52	$5.13	$6.05	--	--
Rotterdam transshipped through Bantry Bay	$8.74 + 1.23	--	--	--	--	$4.28 + 0.78	$5.41 + 0.97
Savings/loss (using Bantry Bay)	-.62 (Milford Haven) -.90 (Rotterdam)		$1.73 to $2.15 (Milford Haven) $1.73 to $2.14 (Rotterdam)	$-.24 to $ .12 (Milford Haven) $-0.33 to 0.06 (Rotterdam)			

Source: Arthur D. Little, Foreign Deepwater Port Developments, 3 vols. (Springfield, Va.: National Technical Information Service, 1971), 3: Table I-1.

As a means to maintain advantages over competitors, and as a profitable new segment of the petroleum industry, terminal operation should attract investors. Investment opportunities are represented by the LOOP and SEADOCK ventures on the Gulf Coast. The East Coast market is also an investment opportunity for which there is not as yet an established project.

Deepwater ports are also attractive to independent terminal operators. A terminal operator can follow the Bantry Bay example set by Gulf Oil. In this case a 1,500-acre site on an island in an Irish bay provided an excellent transshipment terminal. With a ban on refining, Gulf Oil transshipped at 200,000 barrels per day, saving $17 million to $22 million per year. At this rate the terminal paid back its $45 million investment cost in less than three years.[28] Such examples as Bantry Bay (Table 3.14) show that terminals can be profitable quickly.

Although by no means the most important concern to the major oil companies, deepwater terminals are an important element in competition. Terminals have been talked about for the East Coast in New England, in the mid-Atlantic, and as far north as Canada. The Bahamas and Puerto Rico are accessible transshipment sites. Planning is underway at four sites in the Gulf Coast.

In European countries where ports and port regions are highly competitive with one another, dredging ports or moving terminals toward the sea are important economic decisions for regions. Norway, the Netherlands, and Belgium are dependent upon their shipping industry and their port regions. Accordingly, the competition is particularly acute among such ports as Rotterdam, Antwerp, and Amsterdam. The decision to build Bantry Bay and the expansion of Rotterdam are elements in this competition. Despite these competitive circumstances, Bantry Bay provided a pay-back period of less than three years. France is also anxious to develop certain ports with deepwater capability, such as Le Havre and Dunkirk in the north and La Fos in southern France near Marseilles. The lesson from the European experience is that a variety of terminal solutions exists, and that relative to Europe many port investment opportunities exist in the United States. Port development trends are worldwide phenomena and the United States now provides an opportunity in the expansion of this network of ships and terminals.

NOTES

1. More than 1.3 million barrels per day refinery capacity exists between New York and Philadelphia, and more refineries would be built if crude oil ports were constructed. Refining need is

presented by the National Petroleum Council, Factors Affecting U.S. Petroleum Refining (Washington, D.C., May 1973).

2. U.S. Department of Commerce, Maritime Administration, The Economics of Deepwater Terminals (Washington, D.C., 1972), Figure 3, p. 17.

3. The Oil and Gas Journal 72, no. 9 (March 4, 1974): 58-65.

4. Lightering now occurs in sheltered areas of the New York and Delaware bays. For a discussion see Robert R. Nathan Associates, U.S. Deepwater Port Study: Physical Coast and Port Characteristics and Selected Deepwater Port Alternatives, 5 vols. (Springfield, Va.: National Technical Information Service, 1972), 5:164-68.

5. Organization for Economic and Cooperative Development, Maritime Transport 1973 (Paris, 1974), p. 10.

6. Six months' statistics for 1974-75 put tankship tonnage up by nearly 11 percent. John I. Jacobs, World Tanker Fleet Review (London, June 1975).

7. U.S. Department of the Interior, Draft Environmental Impact Statement: Deepwater Ports (Washington, D.C., June 1973), p. 143.

8. H. J. Kaiser Company and Gulf South Research Institute, The Economic Impact of a Louisiana Offshore Oil Port (Baton Rouge, La., 1973), p. 5.

9. Two authors are cited, Zenon S. Zannetos, The Theory of Tankship Rates (Cambridge, Mass.: M.I.T. Press, 1966), and M. A. Adelman, The World Petroleum Market (Baltimore: Johns Hopkins University Press, 1972), Chapter 4.

10. Adelman, op. cit., p. 130.

11. Ibid., pp. 125-30. Incremental ship represents the notion of marginal cost and price whereby one is calculating the cost of a specific vessel for a market that will accept that vessel at a specific but fluctuating price.

12. Organization for Economic and Cooperative Development, op. cit., p. 86.

13. Ibid., p. 52.

14. Jacobs, op. cit.

15. Source for data is Platt's Oilgram Price Service, Platt's Oilgram, 50th ed. (New York: McGraw-Hill, 1975), pp. 28-37.

16. Discussion is based on H. P. Dewry Ltd., The Trading Outlook for Very Large Tankers, no. 32 (London, July 1975).

17. The Petroleum Economist 12, no. 12 (London: Petroleum Press Bureau, December 1974), p. 479.

18. Platt's Oilgram Price Service, op. cit., September 4, 1975.

19. W. L. Nelson, "Tanker-Transportation Costs Decline," The Oil and Gas Journal (June 17, 1974): 67-79.

20. H. P. Dewry Ltd., op. cit., p. 27.

21. Ibid., p. 48.

22. "Business Brief," The Economist (London: August 9, 1975), pp. 48-49.

23. Wall Street Journal, June 5, 1975.

24. Platt's Oilgram Price Service, September 11, 1975.

25. New York Times, October 30, 1975.

26. Sun Oil Company, Corporate Development Group, Analysis of World Tank Ships: 1970 (Philadelphia, August 1971).

27. A comparison of East Coast refinery costs compared to refineries in the Caribbean or Gulf Coast indicated that whatever transport savings exist for East Coast refineries can be offset by tax advantages offered by foreign countries. It should be noted that risk of having tax advantages rescinded is not included. National Petroleum Council, Factors Affecting U.S. Petroleum Refining: A Summary (Washington, D.C., May 1973), Appendix IV, pp. 59-63.

28. Arthur D. Little, Foreign Deepwater Port Developments, 3 vols. (Springfield, Va.: National Technical Information Service, 1971), 3.

FACTORS AFFECTING THE
DEVELOPMENT OF A
PETROCOMPLEX

Among the various ways of measuring the extent of industrial activity caused by a deepwater port is to use the throughput associated with a terminal. Throughput in millions of barrels per day will have a relationship to refining and to petrochemical activity at the onshore end of the terminal pipeline. This activity does not have to occur adjacent to the deepwater terminal site. If the crude oil is transshipped to other ports, or if the terminal is connected to a landward pipeline reaching to the interior, the adjacent onshore activity may be limited to storage.

There is an existing pattern of development that may be strengthened or new centers of petroleum activity may occur. In addition to the actual terminal, it is the magnitude of related secondary development that is a principal concern of the community adjacent to a deepwater terminal. Such a concern involves a mixture of probability, policy, and locational factors.

When a community seeks to attract development, the locational factors and the policy variables can be combined into an industrial program. A method known as industrial complex analysis has been applied to the petrochemical industry. The heart of the analysis is an interindustry matrix of inputs and outputs that would, if located together, form a complex. This complex is evaluated for comparative locational advantage. Walter Isard, Thomas Victorisz, and Eugene Schooler developed this method and applied it to selected aspects of petrochemical development in Puerto Rico as compared to the Gulf Coast.[1] The Arthur D. Little firm became heavily involved in planning for the industrial future of Puerto Rico. Little was the chief consultant to the country for over 20 years and with the chemical background of its founder, the company was quick to promote the island's industrial locational advantages.[2] In developing an industrial program, both the discipline of economics and the promotional ability of knowledgeable consultants and managers can be mobilized to attract suitable development. Both logic and promotion are part of this kind of industrial planning.

As the benefits of industrial development are examined much more closely today, some of the promotional aspects of an industrial program have declined. Now the ecologic and environmental impacts form the evaluative basis of development decisions. It is less the secondary development than the cumulative environmental impacts that must be quantified. More often than not the full range of industrial development possibilities are not examined, since actual development is probabilistic. Rather, a most likely set of development decisions or a range of decisions are examined, in order to assess the air, water, population, and job impact on a community. With characteristic precision, Isard has shown that similar methods of analysis can be applied to economic-ecologic decisions. In his application, comparative cost and activity complex analysis play a part in a case study of a boat marina for Plymouth Bay, which involves some damage to the coastal environment.[3] Little has also applied knowledge of the petroleum industry to an assessment of the onshore effects of deepwater port development.[4] Again the promotional aspect plays a part, since the industrial pattern can be encouraged to develop in an environmentally compatible manner. The Council of Environmental Quality (CEQ) asked Little to examine five sites where port projects were being planned or had been shown to have promise from an industry perspective. These sites were: Machias, Maine (a natural harbor); a vicinity of Sandy Hook near New York harbor on the New Jersey side; Grand Isle, Louisiana; and Freeport, Texas. The changing nature of the industrial-development assessment mission was evident in the CEQ charge:

> Within the framework of the overall CEQ Study,
> Arthur D. Little, Inc. (ADL) was asked to assess
> the onshore, or secondary, effects of deepwater
> terminal development on each of the five areas
> selected as terminal locations. The relative impacts of a terminal in each area affect the relative
> suitability of each area as a terminal site. Relative impacts include the additional industrial development, production, employment, air and
> water pollution, land use, population changes,
> etc. resulting from terminal development. A
> major objective of this effort has been to relate
> these terminal impacts to the normal cumulative
> effects of growth processes on various individual

areas and regions in order to illustrate their apparent capacity to accommodate terminal-related
growth. The selection of sites and the allocation
of oil is somewhat speculative, and the assessment of impacts--both economic and environmen-
tal--are purely illustrative. The results show
what given representative areas could experience
under given circumstances and assumptions, not
necessarily what will happen.[5]

The statement is revealing because it is the impact rather than the
opportunity for development that is being sought; and given this
charge, Little must evaluate what could happen rather than how.
The product of the investigation is, as the statement admits, speculative. Uncertainty is not addressed, no probabilities can be as-
signed to the quantitative impacts, and no policies can be gleaned
from the assessment methodology. The authors recommend disper-
sion of industrial activity to "decongest" the mid-Atlantic on the
basis of the quantities of effluent produced.[6]

After more than two decades of developing analytical techniques
to assess regional development, the outcomes of major decisions are
less, not more, certain. In the past the secondary impacts were examined with better insight because policy and locational factors were
working together. At the same time the environmental aspects were
largely ignored.

The Little Study assessed the degree of industrial concentration that might occur owing to given level of throughput, and used
these levels of activity to assess environmental impacts. Although
the impact quantities are measured in some detail, very little is
understood as to how deepwater ports will develop if sited in the five
locations studied. A speculative study with illustrative results is
useful, but it cannot be examined either for accuracy or as a guide
to planning. It is clear, however, that many of the calculations are
repetitious and meaningless, as they do not represent a probable
future. This harsh conclusion is not a fault of the study, rather it is
symptomatic of how industrial-location factors and policy are at odds
with one another. As there is no policy to dictate what should happen,
Little was forced to assume what might happen based upon strength of
certain locational advantages. The study results would have been improved if the CEQ had put impact analysis in almost any policy context.

LOCATIONAL FACTORS

Given this pessimistic assessment, the industrial planning aspects revert to a more rudimentary form of analysis. A major

consideration of which Little was aware is the relative concentration of the petroleum refining industry. Petroleum refining represents the most important secondary development of a deepwater port.

The Texas area and the Louisiana area served by the Freeport and Grand Isle sites are ideal from an industrial point of view. The terminals would be near the bulk of all coastal refining in the country. The two Jersey sites, one near the Philadelphia refineries and the other near New York, can be explained by proximity to refinery concentration for the entire East Coast. An East Coast site is particularly important because this area represents about 40 percent of the product demand and only about 10 percent of the refinery capacity. Machias, Maine, is not too far to serve such a market because of a natural deepwater harbor, which reduces capital costs. In reviewing a number of cost alternatives, the Maritime Administration found that the pay-back period for a port in Machias, Maine, was 1.0 years to serve a New York/New Jersey terminal. A proposal to dredge the New York harbor would yield a pay-back of 4.2 years.[7] With respect to transshipment, most any terminal located in naturally deep water accessible to the East Coast would be profitable. These harbors exist in Maine, Canada, and the West Indies.

The choice of a representative site is to some degree arbitrary. A low-cost transshipment terminal can be profitable at a relatively low volume throughput, but a $500 million offshore terminal must be either near existing refining capacity, have a pipeline to connect to refineries, or depend upon the development of "grass roots" (developed from scratch) refineries. For the pipeline alternative there should be an existing pipeline with excess capacity or a new pipeline must be built.

The petroleum industry has taken the position that it would prefer to develop additional grass roots refineries in the United States. In the more recent past, refinery expansion has taken place at existing sites, a practice that does not capture the definite economies of scale in refinery construction. Many planned new grass roots refineries are in the range of 100,000 to 300,000 barrels per day capacity. Obsolete refineries that shut down are usually less than 10,000 b/d, but the major companies shut down larger ones.[8] Overall the average new refinery will be larger than existing if permitted to build, but in the meantime the industry will add what capacity it can to present plants. Industry surveys generally show optimistic forecasts of construction, which compared with actual completions indicate a wide divergence. In expressing its views on refinery expansion the National Petroleum Council notes the growing divergence between consumption and refinery construction.[9] The difference is made up by product imports. In calculating refining shortfall, the Council compared trended capacity increases to those increases that would be needed to satisfy product consumption. The trended line yielded capacity at 13.1 million barrels per day (MM b/d) in 1972, 13.7MM b/d in 1975, and 15.6 by 1980. Based on the capacity needed to satisfy domestic consumption, the shortfall was 1.2MM b/d in 1972 and 4.8MM b/d in 1975 and 5.7MM b/d in 1980. In 1972 about 69 percent of the product imports were residual fuel, most of which came from Venezuela. From 1972 to 1975, refining capacity increased to 14.8MM b/d.[10] This increase was more than the trended line (13.7 in 1975), but less than that desired by the industry.

The size of the average refinery has been increasing, but recent expansions represent additions to existing plants rather than grass roots refineries. From 1973 and 1974 capacity has increased for the smaller refining companies--the refiners with the smaller and older plants. The petroleum industry, or at least the major companies, are looking for grass roots expansion. In 1973 the average refinery had a capacity of 58,000 barrels per day. In 1970 the average size was 47,000 b/d and in 1960 it was 33,000 b/d.[11] In 1974 the 17 leading companies represented 80 percent of the capacity, whose average size was 103,000 b/d. Exxon led refining capacity with five refineries whose average size was 250,000 b/d.[12]

Such statistics indicate that new refineries are likely to be large. Their siting will take into account the opportunity to serve the East Coast, the long-term decline in domestic crude oil production, and the environmental requirements that they will have to meet. In terms of ability to pay growing environmental cost, new large refineries will have less of a burden than small plants as a percentage of total investment.[13]

Given the desire of a refiner to locate near the market, and have a secure source of crude, any terminal providing deepwater access will provide an opportunity to site a refinery. The only countertrend would be pressure by producing countries to locate refineries in their nations.[14] Such a trend does spur development of a very large product carrier of the 55,000-80,000 dwt class. For the United States, however, foreign participation in domestic refining is a cheaper solution for both the producing country and the petroleum companies.

What can be sketched out is a desire to locate grass roots refineries somewhat independent of the ability to site an offshore terminal. Conversely, there are transshipment examples, such as Bantry Bay, which are profitable at a low level of throughput without a parallel access to new refinery sites. The relationship between a terminal and a refinery is by no means invariant and can exist independently.

In Europe most deepwater port development is occurring around existing ports, whose outer reaches are becoming the focus of VLCC terminal development. Unlike Bantry Bay, the ports of Rotterdam, Antwerp, Le Havre, La Fos, Dunkirk, and Milford Haven are promoting or permitting industrial agglomeration around regional port centers. On the other hand, Japan is attempting to decongest her ports by decentralizing port expansion.[15] In the United States such port-expansion policies conflict with the expensive and disruptive requirements of dredging existing ports. With the exception of Maine, natural deepwater harbors do not exist along the East Coast.

Local control over refinery-siting decisions would not appear to depend on terminal-siting decisions. Because the Deepwater Port Act gives the governor the right to veto and a right to review terminal facility plans, the decision on a port can be made contingent upon land-use criteria.[16] Moreover, there may be increased ability to review refinery decisions in such cases where refinery and terminal planning are linked, or are required to be linked as a basis for state approval.

PETROCHEMICAL COMPLEX

The locational decisions of the petrochemical industry are associated with refineries. With declining natural gas in the United States, the chemical industry is drawing closer to the use of crude oil and refinery output as raw material for chemical production. The Kaiser/Gulf study indicated that the increased oil from a deepwater terminal was important to the Louisiana petrochemical industry--that without such a terminal no new chemical plants would be located in Louisiana. "Between 1970 and 1980, use of heavy oils in production of ethylene and propylene is expected to increase from 130,000 barrels per day to 780,000 barrels per day in the United States. No new petrochemical plant utilizing natural gas liquids will be built in Louisiana."[17] Waddams reports that between 5.0 to 5.5 percent of petroleum product demand is for chemical production. This proportion is estimated to increase to 11 to 12 percent by the year 2000.[18] At present Waddams reports that 10-15 percent ethylene raw materials (feedstock) and 80-85 percent propylene product come from refineries. In commenting upon the relationship between the petroleum and the chemical industry Waddams notes, "It is apparent from this that, although the possibility exists for a chemical producer to operate independently of the oil industry, other than for the purchase of feedstock, in practice the links tend to remain close. A great deal of petrochemical production is carried out by associate companies of the petroleum industry, and many chemical companies

forge formal links with one of the major oil interests."[19] This relationship is related in a locational sense by the need for raw materials
and the economies of scale in chemical plants. Waddams reports
that normal production capacity for an ethylene and ammonia plant is
about 250,000 to 400,000 tons per year. In the mid-1950s and early
1960s, capacity of a plant was between 30,000 and 70,000 tons. Such
capacity increases draw chemicals and refining together because of
the need for a reliable raw material.[20]

In making a "low-level" assumption regarding one deepwater
port in the mid-Atlantic (at Cape May or Middlesex County, New
Jersey) Little assumed petrochemical development would use as raw
materials 12 percent of refinery capacity by 1985 and 17 percent by
2000.[21] By 1985, 460,000 b/d refinery capacity devoted to chemical
production would be added to existing sites if the terminal were located near Delaware Bay at Cape May County and 150,000 b/d capacity would be added if the terminal were located near the New York
harbor at Middlesex County.[22] Under the "high-import level" refinery capacity expands by a factor of eight and there are 25 petrochemical complexes rather than six estimated with the low level. This
high-level estimate would appear unreasonable.

In evaluating the attractiveness of the mid-Atlantic, Little considered the declining advantage the Gulf Coast would have as the
chemical-producing region, as the nation moves to heavier petroleum
raw materials with an East Coast port. Chemical manufacturers
could move closer to demand and save on transport cost. This relative shift was not believed to be dramatic because of the infrastruc-
ture and labor pool advantages of the Gulf.[23]

Oil companies own much of the refinery production for chemicals and have captured about 50 percent of the primary petrochemical manufacture. In the more variable, difficult, and lower-volume
chemical markets the oil companies' share is less, representing 24
percent of the intermediate petrochemical market but 13 percent of
the total derivative market.[24] Reports from the seventy-ninth meeting of the American Institute of Chemical Engineers indicate that all
new ethylene capacity would come from refinery output and somewhat
the same picture was drawn for propylene and benzene.[25] If, as it
appears, the raw material source is the major determinant of primary chemical-manufacture location decisions, it is likely that
petrochemical complexes will locate on the East Coast if crude is
imported through a deepwater terminal. Chemical manufacture is
a worldwide industry, and the growth rate in the United States has
been predicted to be less than the rest of the world.[26] Refinery output of chemical feedstocks in Middle East producing areas is apt to
be the cheapest source of raw material for the chemical industry.

At the same time it is assumed that petrochemical plants will move toward deepwater terminals in order to secure raw material, it can also be shown that the Middle East is a profitable export location. This locational advantage is based on cheap natural gas. For example, an M.I.T. study calculated that 1 billion cubic feet of natural gas could be made available in Saudi Arabia for the production of liquid natural gas (LNG).[27] The market for LNG would include the United States and Japan. Local Middle East markets are not large enough to use large quantities of natural gas, which is now wasted.[28] Despite the Middle East's advantage, it would not be expected to capture a large share of the market owing to the incremental cost of moving downstream processes away from the existing market.

POST-1970 REFINERY AND PETROCHEMICAL SITES

The more recent siting decisions (see Table 4.1 and Table 4.2) have emphasized Gulf Coast refinery and petrochemical sites. Many proposals to site on the East Coast have not borne fruit. The exception is Nova Scotia, where Canadian deepwater access has contributed to the location of two grass roots refineries. More refineries are planned for the east coast of Canada. East Coast U.S. sites have been sought by the industry but have met with local opposition. Several refinery proposals and the ICOL refinery north of New Orleans are partially based upon the utility fuel oil market rather than cracking for gasoline. As with most of the Gulf sites, the ICOL site will have the potential use of deepwater facilities at the LOOP project in Louisiana.

Petrochemical locations tend to be tied even closer to existing refinery centers than grass roots refinery expansion. Most increased capacity in refineries has come from expansions at existing sites, and the petrochemical activity may logically follow this trend. At least one chemical manufacturer is in a position of entering the refining business in order to secure raw material for chemicals.

If Canadian refinery and Gulf Coast deepwater port sites move ahead as planned, then these two centers may supply the East Coast with products and crude oil. It is likely that both refining centers will attract petrochemical activity.

SEADOCK AND LOOP PROJECTS

The level of throughput for LOOP and SEADOCK in 1980 is forecast well below the crude oil needs of refineries in the proposed

TABLE 4.1

Recent Refinery and Terminal Sitings Serving U.S. Market

Location	Process Unit Size	Acreage Acquired	Crude Access	Transportation
Refinery: Corpus Christie, Texas (along ship channel)	65,000-125,000 b/d on 210 acres	705 acres	Near term: Middle East Long term: Mexico or Alaska	Near term: Caribbean transshipment Long term: Deep-water port Freeport or Corpus Christie
Refinery: Lovington, New Mexico	37,000 b/d on 75 acres	640 acres (90-year lease)	Domestic via pipeline	Pipeline
Refinery: Garyville, Louisiana (on the Mississippi)	200,000 b/d	2,500 acres	Saudi Arabia	Near term: trans-shipment Caribbean Long term: Project LOOP and tug barge up Mississippi to refinery site
LNG terminal: Cove Point, Maryland (on Chesapeake Bay) (proposed)	Four tanks and piping on 300 acres	1,000 acre site with one-third mile buffer zone adjacent to operations	LNG from Algeria	125,000 cubic meter LNG tanker (nominal 750,000 barrel)
Refinery: Come-By-Chance, Nova Scotia	100,000 b/d (more refin-eries planned)	330 acres	Middle East supplied by British Petroleum	Very large crude carrier
Refinery: Joliet, Illinois	160,000 b/d 600 acres	1,200 acres	Alberta, Canada; New Mexico; Wyoming; and offshore Louisiana	3 pipeline systems
Refinery: Alliance, Louisiana (Plaquemine Parish)	150,000 b/d	700 acres	Offshore Louisiana	Pipeline
Refinery: Port Tupper, Nova Scotia	150,000 b/d	n.a.	Middle East	Very large crude carrier
Refinery: Cherry Point, Washington	98,000 b/d	n.a.	n.a.	n.a.
Port Allen, Pennsylvania	36,000 b/d	n.a.	n.a.	n.a.

Note: All decisions have resulted in completed grass roots development except where noted. (n.a.--data not available.)

Source: Oil and Gas Journal (October 1972 - April 1975).

market areas.[29] SEADOCK expects throughput of 1.6 million barrels per day and LOOP 1.265 million barrels, as noted in Table 4.3.

SEADOCK's primary market area consists of coastal refineries from Corpus Christie, Texas, to Lake Charles, Louisiana. Refinery capacity in barrels per day in 1972 consists of: Corpus Christi (340,000), Galveston-Houston (1,460,000), Beaumont-Port Arthur (1,291,000), and Lake Charles, Louisiana (306,000). SEADOCK estimates of 1975 refining capacity in Table 4.3 do not quite include all of the above refineries, as their estimate of 3.318 million barrel capacity indicates.[30] Nevertheless, from this 3,318,000 barrel total SEADOCK members in Texas and Lake Charles have a refinery capacity of 1.516 million barrels. Planned expansion by 1978 is an estimated 450,000 barrels in Texas by SEADOCK members, and 217,000 barrels in Texas by nonmembers. Refineries served by SEADOCK can very well be limited to members to attain the estimated 1980 throughput. In addition to these coastal facilities, there is a secondary market area of inland Texas refineries and refineries in Oklahoma, Kansas, southwestern Missouri, and the western third of Arkansas.[31]

The competitive edge of SEADOCK depends upon continued refinery expansion in Texas and the need for overseas crude oil. Regardless of future petroleum consumption, it is estimated that there will be a significant shortfall of domestic crude to serve existing refinery capacity in the Texas and Lake Charles area. In other words, more foreign crude will be needed just to serve existing refineries. Adding 1975 capacity (3.318 million barrels) and 1978 expansion (667,000 barrels), and then subtracting estimated domestic production for these refineries in 1980 (2.118 million barrels) yields the shortfall of crude (1.87 million barrels). Although the above S. H. Clark domestic crude production estimates for SEADOCK are definitely on the low side, there is some likelihood of a domestic crude oil shortfall. A lower estimate might consider refinery expansion cancellation, if demand did not materialize. Even without a shortfall, Texas coastal refining is the most likely to export products to the rest of the nation. Taking into consideration that members of SEADOCK can compare domestic versus foreign crude oil price options and the likelihood of some domestic shortfall, SEADOCK throughput estimate is reasonable for 1980.

Later some 1985 throughput scenarios will be examined linking Gulf Coast and East Coast petroleum import needs. These point out that in the absence of an East Coast port, a primary function of SEADOCK is to supply refineries on the Gulf Coast in order to deliver petroleum products on the East Coast.

The demand for petroleum on the East Coast, the Alaskan crude oil trade, and the potential for crude oil finds in the Gulf of

TABLE 4.2

Recent Petrochemical Sitings Serving the U.S. Market

Location	Process Unit Size	Size	Raw Material Access
Bayport, Texas	400 million lbs./year polypropylene	153 acres; occupies one-third of site	Nearby refineries
Channel View, Texas (proposed)	1.3 billion lbs./year ethylene 800 million lbs./year propylene 200 million lbs./year butadiene	n.a.	Increased ARCO refinery output
Tulsa, Oklahoma (Arkansas River Navigation Channel)	425,000 ton/year ammonia 600,000 ton/year urea	n.a.	Natural gas feedstock
Ponce, Puerto Rico	775 million lbs./year ethylene (total output 3 billion lbs./year all chemicals)	n.a.	40-45,000 b/d naphtha from Western Hemisphere (Venezuela?)

Note: All sitings are new plants except where noted (n.a.--data not available).
Source: Oil and Gas Journal (October 1972-April 1975).

TABLE 4.3

Volume and Capacity--SEADOCK and LOOP
(thousands of barrels per day and millions of dollars)

	SEADOCK	LOOP
Estimated throughput		
1980	1,600[a]	1,265.0[b]
1985	1,900	1,870.0[c]
Design capacity		
1980	2,000	1,400.0
Future	2,500-4,000	3,400.0
Capacity of refineries in service area (1975)	3,318	3,288.4
Capital cost[d]		
By 1980	$659	$348
Ultimate	865	738

[a]1,400M b/d from SEADOCK shareholders and 200M b/d from others.
[b]855M b/d from LOOP shareholders and 410M b/d from others.
[c]918M b/d from LOOP shareholders and 952M b/d from others.
[d]Estimated in millions of dollars in year spent.
Sources: LOOP, Inc., Application for License, 22 vols. (Washington, D.C.: U.S. Coast Guard, 1975); SEADOCK, Inc., Application for License, 5 vols. (Washington, D.C.: U.S. Coast Guard, 1975); "Response to Six Inquiries in Telex from Commandant of Coast Guard to LOOP dated January 14, 1976" (Washington, D.C.: U.S. Department of Transportation, 1976).

Mexico tend to converge on the need for Gulf Coast refining. Coastal
refineries are closer to markets, given no similar expansion on the
East Coast, and Gulf Coast refineries have the ability to be served
by widely dispersed crude oil production centers. With declining
domestic inland production, SEADOCK reduces transport cost of
overseas crude oil, which in turn reinforces refinery expansion
along the coast. As refineries expand on the Texas Coast, chemical
plants are likely to locate there to obtain their supplies.

The LOOP project is only partly oriented to the Gulf Coast and
relies more on pipelines to serve the mid-West. Shareholder capacity is somewhat less than SEADOCK (855,000 barrels). As shown in
the following map, the principal pipeline connections are the St.
James pipeline (insert) that takes crude from the Clovelly salt domes;
the Capline pipeline that extends from St. James, Louisiana, to
Patoka, Illinois; and a series of pipelines extending north, east, and
west. By 1980, Capline is expected to have a 1.25 million barrel
capacity. Through this pipeline the LOOP port may reach a market
of 3,288,400 barrels of refining capacity. The project can be further
linked with 776,200 barrels via pipeline and 786,400 barrels by river
transport.[32] LOOP can provide these mid-West refineries with
crude oil as production declines in the major producing states.

LOOP's advantage in serving the mid-West market is due to the
existing imbalance in refining capacity and crude production. With a
crude oil shortfall, LOOP can serve this market better than existing
pipeline connections. LOOP would then be more oriented to serving
refineries and mid-West markets, while SEADOCK would be the
means to serve the East Coast. In addition to keeping mid-West refineries supplied, Louisiana refineries can use LOOP crude oil and
ship products up the Mississippi River. H. J. Kaiser estimates that
by 1980 the mid-West would require 3 million barrels a day to keep
refineries operating there. From this total, 1 million barrels a day
would come from foreign sources. Also projected is an additional
need of 900,000 barrels a day in products not refined in the mid-
West, but which could come from LOOP.[33] Additional products
mean that more refineries could be located in Louisiana to serve
both mid-West and East Coast product demand.

As both SEADOCK and LOOP expect diminished natural gas
supply for chemicals, refinery decisions in Texas and Louisiana are
likely to alter chemical plant decisions. The engineering firm of
Dames and Moore forecast that 18 percent of refinery runs will go
to chemicals in Texas if natural gas supply is eliminated. The
Kaiser report assumes that for Louisiana all chemical plants will
be built on the basis that refinery product is available.

MAP 4.1

LOOP Pipeline Access to Refineries

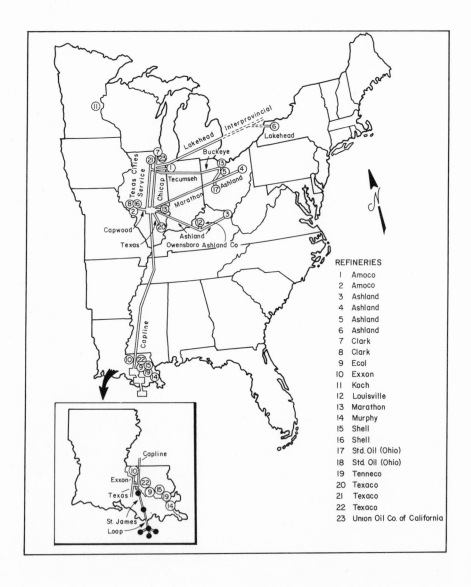

REFINERIES

1	Amoco
2	Amoco
3	Ashland
4	Ashland
5	Ashland
6	Ashland
7	Clark
8	Clark
9	Ecol
10	Exxon
11	Koch
12	Louisville
13	Marathon
14	Murphy
15	Shell
16	Shell
17	Std. Oil (Ohio)
18	Std. Oil (Ohio)
19	Tenneco
20	Texaco
21	Texaco
22	Texaco
23	Union Oil Co. of California

Source: LOOP Inc., Application for License, 22 vols. (Washington, D.C.: U.S. Coast Guard, 1975).

DEEPWATER PORT THROUGHPUT SCENARIOS

As Chapter 2 challenged the high import estimates of the past, a set of revised estimates can be the basis for taking a closer look at port options. From Chapter 2, a revised estimate of 1985 consumption was forecast. Total consumption growing at 2 percent and 3.5 percent are compared against two supply options, whose supply demand balances both yield imports of 9.1 million barrels. This estimate in Table 4.4 may be a plausible forecast, but given the range of supply and demand options, lower levels of imports rather than higher levels would be expected as a most likely forecast.

These import levels are then allocated to District I, whereby New England accounts for 20 percent of the East Coast market. District I production is ignored. Total domestic production has no effect on waterborne East Coast consumption nor affects the source of these imports. Consequently, only two estimates of East Coast waterborne imports are shown in Table 4.4. Total foreign waterborne imports are estimated at 8 million barrels and overland Canadian imports at 1.1 million barrels. Total East Coast consumption is greater than total foreign waterborne imports, which defines what must be made up by Gulf Coast exports to the East Coast.

Turning to Table 4.5, the 8 million barrel (1985) imports are allocated to three crude oil terminal sites. The total throughput crude is estimated at 1.9 million barrels for SEADOCK, 2 million barrels at LOOP, and 1.1 million barrels at an offshore site in New Jersey. The actual crude throughput is 5 million barrels to allow for a 3 million barrel import of residual fuel oil mostly to the East Coast. As noted in the table, the potential existing refining capacity that would be served by such terminals includes Texas coast refining, Louisiana coast, and Capline pipeline refineries in the mid-West and those refineries located near Philadelphia and New York.

If neither a port nor refineries were built to serve the New York-Philadelphia area, offshore sites in Maine, Canada, or the Bahamas are candidates for the 1.1 million barrel crude oil needs. If none of these sites took up the slack, then SEADOCK or LOOP might supply refineries on the Gulf Coast for transshipment to the East Coast. Consequently, the East Coast site is arbitrary and not based on any active deepwater port proposals.

These sites require additional capital. In Texas, pipelines would be required, or what is more likely, the crude oil would be transshipped by barge. SEADOCK has estimated pipeline cost of $190 million to serve the Houston/Baytown, Texas City, and Beaumont/Port Arthur areas.[34] In Louisiana, Capline would have to be expanded to the planned 1.25 million barrels per day. For the coast of New Jersey, a site near New York or Philadelphia could be

TABLE 4.4

Domestic Production and Consumption Assumptions for Alternative Port Analysis

(millions of barrels of daily oil equivalent)

| | | | 1985--Total U.S. | | P.A.D. District I[b] | | | |
| | | | 2% Demand Growth | 3.5% Demand Growth | New England | | Rest of East Coast | |
	1970	1973			2%	3.5%	2%	3.5%
Total consumption	14.7	17.25	21.9	26.0	1.8	2.1	6.8	8.1
Total production	11.3	11.05	12.8	16.9	0	0	0	0
Total imports	3.4	6.2	9.1	9.1	1.8	2.1	6.8	8.1
Total waterborne imports (including shipments between districts)	2.7	5.1	8.0	8.0	1.8	2.1	5.5[a]	6.8[a]

[a]Assumes 1.3MM b/d pipeline refined products to East Coast with no pipeline expansion.
[b]Petroleum Administrative District.

Note: Based on Table 3.14, where total waterborne imports remain at 8MM b/d for the United States. It is assumed that West Coast demand will be made up by domestic continental and Alaskan trade. District II (mid-West) will be made up by domestic production, Canadian imports, and Gulf Coast imports. District I is assumed to be 39 percent of total U.S. market, 80 percent of which is mid- and south-Atlantic, and 20 percent is New England.

Sources: Table 3.14; Robert R. Nathan Associates, U.S. Deepwater Port Study, 5 vols. (Springfield, Va.: National Technical Information Service, 1972), 2:66; Committee on Science and Astronautics, U.S. Congress, House, Energy Facts, 93rd Cong., 1st session, November 1973, p. 349.

TABLE 4.5

Offshore Terminal Representative Port Proposals, 1985-90: Impact Analysis
(throughput and refinery capacity in million barrels daily)

	Freeport, Texas	La Fourche, Louisiana	Ocean County, New Jersey
Market served[a]	Coastal Texas: Corpus Christi to Lake Charles	Louisiana coastal and midwest via Capline pipeline	Philadelphia area and New York area refineries
Existing refinery[b] and pipeline capacity served	3.985	4.851	1.3
Total waterborne[c] foreign crude and product import estimate: 1985	Gulf Coast 3.9 (crude only; no products)	East Coast 1.1 (crude) 3.0 (product-- mainly residual)	
Estimated offshore terminal crude throughput	1.9	2.0[d]	1.1
Additional transportation facilities	Additional pipeline capacity: Corpus Christi to Lake Charles (or coastal barge)	Expand Capline and lay parallel pipeline	Crude pipeline parallel to product lines Philadelphia-New York, pipeline from terminal (or coastal barge)

[a]Based upon offshore terminal proposals of SEADOCK and LOOP. Ocean County is hypothetical, based upon criteria of refinery concentration and safety distance from existing harbors.

[b]Uses existing refinery capacity (about 1973) for the New York-Philadelphia area. For Louisiana and Texas, refinery capacity is based upon LOOP and SEADOCK projects.

[c]Assumes total imports of 8MM b/d, excluding Canadian and Alaskan (domestic waterborne).

[d]Based upon 0.75MM b/d to Louisiana refineries and 1.25MM b/d to midWest via Capline capacity at 1.25MM b/d.

Sources: National Petroleum Council, U.S. Petroleum and Gas Transportation Capacities (Washington, D.C., 1967); National Petroleum News, Factbook (New York: McGraw-Hill, 1974); Oil and Gas Journal (March 4, 1974); H. J. Kaiser/Gulf South Research Institute, The Economic Impact of a Louisiana Offshore Oil Port (Baton Rouge, La., 1973); SEADOCK, Inc., Application for License, 5 vols. (Washington, D.C.: U.S. Coast Guard, 1975); LOOP, Inc., Application for License, 22 vols. (Washington, D.C.: U.S. Coast Guard, 1975).

served by pipeline, which is less risky with respect to spills. If the site were offshore a considerable distance north of Delaware Bay or south of New York harbor, the least cost alternative is to transship crude by barge. Environmental concerns could dictate a complete pipeline system with a port location some distance from existing harbor entrances.

From the viewpoint of state and local government, several interdependent decisions can be identified. These decisions are described as a matrix of alternative actions in Table 4.6. The matrix applies to the East Coast on the assumption that both SEADOCK and LOOP will be built. The matrix consists of three decisions: (1) "grass roots" refining expansion; (2) 50 percent expansion of refinery capacity at existing sites by 1985; and (3) limited expansion of refinery capacity at existing sites. These decisions reflect a descending order of development. As a matter of policy, it is assumed that no grass roots refineries are permitted in the mid-Atlantic, but one option permits such refineries in New England. Such a policy would be consistent with a conservation perspective of the New York to Washington conurbation.

TABLE 4.6

Matrix of Alternative Actions for East Coast State Governments[a]

East Coast Refineries	Terminals		
	Gulf Coast[c]	Mid-Atlantic	Gulf, Mid-Atlantic, and New England
No grass roots refineries-- 50% expansion at existing mid-Atlantic sites[b]	A	D	G[d]
No grass roots refineries-- limited expansion at existing mid-Atlantic sites[b]	B	E	H[d]
Grass roots refineries in New England--expansion at 50% for existing mid-Atlantic sites	C	F	I

[a]All options assume residual will arrive from Venezuela by tanker.

[b]Commodity flows between mid-Atlantic and New England are ignored and considered part of secondary distribution.

[c]Gulf Coast terminal for offshore crude is considered to be equivalent to a West Indian or Canadian offshore terminal.

[d]Under these options the offshore terminal in New England handles products for both New England and the mid-Atlantic.

Source: Tables 4.4 and 4.5.

These three policy prototypes are arrayed against terminal location siting decisions. The most likely terminal site is the Gulf
Coast, the second site is the mid-Atlantic, and a third site is New
England, probably Maine. It is assumed that such ports are presented in order of acceptability, so that if the Gulf site is approved
then the mid-Atlantic site would follow. Whether the New England
site is more difficult to approve than the mid-Atlantic is difficult to
assess.* The matrix is presented as a 3 x 3 array of decisions. A
fuller array of grass roots and terminal decisions would show a 4 x 4
matrix: the East Coast grass roots refinery and the Gulf Coast and
New England--but no mid-Atlantic terminal options are considered.

The outcomes from the policy option/terminal locations are
examined in Table 4.7. The outcomes are expressed in terms of
commodity flows. These flows are presented as shifts in market
shares of one origin-destination compared to all other origins and
destinations. All shifts are from a 1971 estimated base calculated
from several sources. The south Atlantic states of Georgia, North
and South Carolina, and Florida are omitted. New England and the
mid-Atlantic commodity flows are estimated separately. East Coast
imports are estimated in terms of where the oil is coming from
rather than where it is produced.

For the mid-Atlantic crude oil shipments direct from the Middle
East increase for all options except A-C. For these options crude
oil will come from a transshipment point, and will increase only
slightly if crude refining expansion is limited. With refineries in
New England, a mid-Atlantic terminal can provide transshipment to
New England and consequently throughput may be greater than what
limited mid-Atlantic refinery expansion might dictate. Product imports increase only with alternative B, where refinery expansion is
limited and no terminal serves the East Coast.

For New England only grass roots refining and a terminal will increase direct Middle East shipments of crude, but grass roots refining will increase transshipped crude if no terminal is built. If no
grass roots refining were allowed, then a terminal decision could
possibly result in a product terminal as shown by alternatives G and
H. Product imports decline for existing mid-Atlantic ports if either
a terminal is approved or grass roots refineries are allowed.

---

*Past attempts by industry to site terminals in Maine, New
Hampshire, and Delaware have been unsuccessful. Local opposition was expressed in Machias and Eastport, Maine; opposition was
received from state officials in Delaware, and local opposition (but
gubernatorial support) was evident in New Hampshire.

TABLE 4.7

Schematic of Alternative Actions--Commodity Flows in Shares of Movement/Shares of Commodity Flows Under Alternatives, 1985

Destination	1971 (Estimated)	A	B	C	D	E	F	G	H	I
Mid-Atlantic										
Via: Product pipeline from Gulf Coast	10%	About same	Declines slightly	About same	Declines	Declines	Declines	Declines	Declines	Declines
Crude shipped direct from Middle East and Venezuela	20%	Declines	Declines	Declines	Increases greatly	Increases	Increases greatly	Increases greatly	Increases	Increases greatly
Shipped or transshipped crude--Gulf, West Indies, and Canada	16%	Increases greatly	Increases slightly	Increases	Declines	Declines slightly	Declines	Increases greatly	Declines slightly	Declines
Residual from Venezuela	32%	About same	About same	About same	About same	Same	Same	Same	Same	Same
Product by tanker-- Gulf Coast or foreign	22%	Declines slightly	Increases	Increases	Declines slightly	Same	Declines slightly	Declines slightly	Increases slightly	Same
Total	100%									
New England										
Via: Middle East or Venezuelan crude	0	0	0	0	0	0	0	0	0	Increases slightly
Shipped or transshipped crude	0	0	0	Increases greatly	0	0	Increases greatly	(May have product terminal)		0
Residual from Venezuela	30%	Same	Same	Same	Same	Same	Same	Same	Same	Same
Product by tanker-- Gulf or foreign	70%	Same	Same	Declines	Same	Same	Declines	Declines	Declines	Declines greatly
Total	100%									

Note: Assumes a product market share of 60% mid-Atlantic, 20% New England, and 20% south Atlantic.

Sources: H. J. Kaiser Company and Gulf South Research Institute, The Economic Impact of a Louisiana Offshore Oil Port (Baton Rouge, La., 1973), Tables 7, 12, 13; National Petroleum Council, U.S. Petroleum and Gas Transportation Capacities (Washington, D.C., 1967), pp. 33, 71; and Arthur D. Little, Potential Onshore Effects of Deepwater Oil Terminal-Related Industrial Development, 5 vols. (Springfield, Va.: National Technical Information Service, 1973), 5: Appendix II.

Some of the impacts of the alternatives are illustrated in Table 4.8, for three terminal sites. For the county of Brazoria, Texas, and for La Fourche Parish, Louisiana, it is assumed that the areas adjacent to the deepwater terminal will increase their refining and petrochemical activity.[35] The assumptions are based on a scenario whereby refining capacity is about 80 percent of consumption of products at a 2 percent growth rate. This growth rate is modest and the 80 percent share criterion maintains domestic refining (districts I, II, and III) at 1973 share of market. No doubt there will be some pressure from overseas to locate refineries in producing countries. By using these rules of thumb, nationwide refinery expansion would increase by 2.7 million barrels.

None of the refinery expansion would be built on the East Coast, as a most likely assumption. The throughput at SEADOCK may be taken up by expanding refineries along the Texas coast. Refineries could also be built in Louisiana to take crude oil not sent through Capline. These possibilities are shown in Table 4.8, where future growth in petroleum consumption results in refinery construction in Texas and Louisiana coastal areas. Additional crude needed to replace dwindling domestic reserves is delivered through three offshore ports, but the East Coast site serves existing refineries and most of the LOOP crude oil is used by existing mid-West refineries.

As a result of this particular scenario (Table 4.8), the United States would only need one large refinery per year at about 270,000 barrels per day. There would be a 50 percent expansion of refining in Texas and Louisiana as a secondary development. Much less new development would occur if the East Coast allowed refineries, as shown in one of the three East Coast refinery options. Almost all chemical plant construction would follow refinery construction.

With 8 million barrels of waterborne imports a year and 5 million barrels of crude imported, current siting decisions favor a Gulf Coast expansion in refining. Expansion would be less likely in the mid-West and the East Coast, as about 2.35 million barrels per day of replacement crude oil would be needed to serve existing refineries. West Coast needs would be served by Alaskan, Indonesian, and Mexican oil, and Western domestic fields.

The local impacts of terminal expansion are not overwhelming, as noted in Table 4.8. Brazoria and La Fourche areas receive one refinery and one chemical plant.

With the East Coast policy of expansion restricted to existing sites, there would be no refinery expansion at the coastal New Jersey county. The value of the illustration is to indicate that onshore development is probabilistic and amenable to land-use controls. There is a limit to development based upon the linked chain of intermediate processes whereby products reach the consumer. A limited throughput reduces the possible degree of agglomeration that can take place.

TABLE 4.8

Additional Capacity to Year 1985
(million barrels per day [MM b/d])

Impact Areas	Brazoria County, Texas	La Fourche Parish, Louisiana	A Coastal County, New Jersey
Analytical assumptions: refineries	All crude imports parallel net addition in refining capacity 1.9MM b/d	750MM b/d parallel to net addition to Louisiana refineries	1.1MM b/d; no net addition to the coastal county adjacent to terminal
Potential sites of new refineries	Corpus Christi to Port Arthur	Inland near Capline and Louisiana coastal zone line (Lake Charles to Baton Rouge to Mississippi state line)	At existing sites Philadelphia, and New York metropolitan area in New Jersey
Policy assumptions	Industry will select sites based on convenience and environmental criteria	Industry will select sites based on convenience and environmental criteria	Expansion restricted to existing locations
Policy output	Additional refinery capacity in Brazoria transshipment to other Texas refinery centers; and grass roots refineries (coast)	Additional refinery capacity in La Fourche parish--transshipment to Mississippi River; and grass roots refineries (coast or inland)	No grass roots refineries; alternatives D and E most likely
New refinery construction	400,000 b/d refinery (20% share)*	100,000 b/d refinery (13% share)*	No refinery in Ocean County*
Petro-chemical activity	One plant*	One plant*	None*

*Refers to specific site as example.
Source: Tables 4.4-4.7.

TABLE 4.9

Illustrative Offshore and Coastal Facility Requirements

Location and Throughput	Freeport 1.9MM b/d	La Fourche 2.0MM b/d	East Coast (New Jersey) 1.1MM b/d
Tanker berths[a] (avg. vessel 250,000 dwt)	4	4	2 to 3
Intermediate[b] tank storage capacity (million barrels)	15×10^6 (25 tanks)	15×10^6 (25 tanks)	12×10^6 (20 tanks)
Land requirements[c] for tank farm	130 acres	130 acres	110 acres
Transshipment[d] berths for coastal barge	Vary according to system used-- not more than 3	None-- assume pipeline	Vary according to system used-- not more than 2

[a]With an average vessel size of 250,000 dwt, the number of ship callings determine the number of berths under the condition that average service time per ship was 30 hours. Each day vessel waiting time was assumed to be equal to $50,000 and the cost of an additional berth was estimated at $4 million. Sources for assumptions and calculations are Robert R. Nathan, and Jan de Weille and Anandarup Ray.

[b]Based upon Robert R. Nathan, vol. 3, Table 17. Assumes 600,000 barrel tanks.

[c]Assumes 150,000 barrels per acre from Robert R. Nathan and W. L. Nelson. Actual land use depends upon land costs and buffer-zone requirements.

[d]Robert R. Nathan.

Sources: Robert R. Nathan Associates, U.S. Deepwater Port Study, 5 vols. (Springfield, Va.: National Technical Information Service, 1972), 3:255, 262-66, 264, 445; Jan de Weille and Anandarup Ray, "The Optimum Port Capacity," Journal of Transport Economics and Policy (September 1974); W. L. Nelson, "Cost of Refineries," Oil and Gas Journal (July 29, 1974): 162.

Some of the other terminal investment needs are dependent upon the transport system. As shown in Table 4.9, the levels of throughput require several berths for tankers, intermediate storage tanks, land for such tanks, and possibly barge transshipment berths. Tanker berth needs are presumed to involve a trade-off between the value of time and the additional capital cost of the berth. At the assumed values, four berths would be needed for each Gulf site. In present weak tanker markets, and given that the terminal is not dedicated (total tanker arrivals are unknown), the additional savings of the extra berth is somewhat overstated. Both SEADOCK and LOOP plan to have about four berths initially and then expand to six buoys.

Tank requirements do not include those at the refinery site, and would require more storage with a transshipment arrangement than with pipeline access. The land requirements based upon the Nathan study were not land-cost dependent. W. L. Nelson has shown that land use for refineries is very sensitive to cost and up to a point traded off for construction techniques.[36] It is difficult to be precise on land use because cost of land is associated with urbanization and consequently it is likely that buffer-zone requirements will increase with urbanization.

The LOOP project has an abundance of storage capacity with eight 4-million-barrel salt dome cavities at Clovelly. SEADOCK is planned with 28 tanks with 22 million barrels total storage capacity. The SEADOCK project has acquired 860 acres of land and can expand the tank farm to 37 tanks.

NOTES

1. Walter Isard and Eugene Schooler, Location Factors in the Petrochemical Industry (Washington, D.C.: Office of Technical Services, U.S. Department of Commerce, 1955); Walter Isard and Thomas Victorisz, "Industrial Complex Analysis and Regional Development with Particular Reference to Puerto Rico," Papers and Proceedings of the Regional Science Association I (1955); Walter Isard, Methods of Regional Analysis: An Introduction to Regional Science (Cambridge, Mass.: M.I.T. Press, 1960).

2. Paul Dickson, Think Tanks (New York: Atheneum, 1971), p. 190.

3. Walter Isard, Charles L. Choquill, John Kissin, Richard H. Seyforth, and Richard Tatlock, Ecologic-Economic Analysis for Regional Development (New York: The Free Press, 1972).

4. Arthur D. Little, Potential Onshore Effects of Deepwater Oil Terminal-Related Industrial Development, 5 vols. (Springfield, Va.: National Technical Information Service, 1973).

5. Ibid., 1:1-3.

6. Ibid., pp. 1-56.

7. U.S. Department of Commerce, The Economics of Deep-water Terminals (Washington, D.C.: U.S. Government Printing Office, 1972), Table 19, p. 42.

8. Trends in refinery expansion are presented in Oil and Gas Journal (February 5, 1973): 56.

9. National Petroleum Council, Factors Affecting U.S. Petroleum Refining: A Summary (Washington, D.C., 1973).

10. Leo R. Aalund, "Refinery Capacity Registers Largest 'nickel and dime' Jump in History," Oil and Gas Journal (April 1, 1974): 76-79. Leo R. Aalund, "Building by Small Refiners Boosts U.S. Refining Total," Oil and Gas Journal (March 24, 1975): 13-16.

11. National Petroleum Council, op. cit., p. 18.

12. Oil and Gas Journal (April 1, 1975): 79

13. Environmental Protection Agency, Background Information for Proposed New Source Performance Standards, 3 vols. (Research Triangle Park, N.C., 1974), 3: 101-07.

14. "New Trend Toward Construction in Producing Areas," Petroleum Economist (September 1974).

15. Betrand L. De Frondeville, Foreign Deepwater Port Developments, 3 vols. (Washington, D.C.: Corps of Engineers, 1971).

16. U.S. Congress, House, Deepwater Port Act of 1974, H.R. 10701, p. 66.

17. H. J. Kaiser Company and Gulf South Research Institute, The Economic Impact of a Louisiana Offshore Oil Port (Baton Rouge, La., 1973), p. 41.

18. A. L. Waddams, Chemicals from Petroleum (New York: John Wiley and Sons, 1973), p. 301; Arthur D. Little reports that in 1970, 3.5 percent of product demand in the United States was used by the chemical industry. Little, op. cit., 5:5; SEADOCK Application for License cites 7.0 percent (1971) to 7.9 percent (1973) from U.S. Department of Interior, Mineral Industry Surveys: Crude Petroleum, Petroleum Products, and Natural Gas.

19. Waddams, op. cit., p. 264.

20. Ibid., p. 9.

21. Little, op. cit., 2:2-10.

22. Ibid., 2:12, 16.

23. Ibid., 5:17, 18.

24. Ibid., 5:5-22.

25. "Large Petrochem Supply Seen Temporary," Oil and Gas Journal (March 24, 1975): 18-20.

26. Ted Wett, "Petrochems Face Tight Feedstock Year," Oil and Gas Journal (March 11, 1974): 73-79. Ted Wett, "Scarce, Costly Feed May Bill Petrochem Expansion," Oil and Gas Journal (August 6, 1973): 19-22.

27. William W. Seifert, Mohammed A. Bakr, and M. Ali Kettani, eds., Energy and Development: A Case Study (Cambridge, Mass.: M.I.T. Press, 1973).

28. The agglomeration tendency of refining and petrochemicals is shown in Western Germany. A pipeline from Trieste has also been a factor in a southward drift of Germany's refining capacity in H. J. Kuhl, "Structure of Petroleum Refining in Western Germany," and A. M. Gemassmer, "The Petrochemical Industry in the Federal Republic of Germany," Journal of the Institute of Petroleum (London, November 1970).

29. SEADOCK, Inc., Application for License, 5 vols. (Washington, D.C.: U.S. Coast Guard, 1975); LOOP, Inc., Application for License, 22 vols. (Washington, D.C.: U.S. Coast Guard, 1975).

30. SEADOCK, op. cit., 6:3-12.

31. Ibid., 6:3-26. SEADOCK retained S. H. Clark Associates to evaluate future refinery and crude oil forecasts.

32. LOOP, op. cit., 1:97.

33. Ibid., 1:33-36.

34. SEADOCK, op. cit., 6:2-7.

35. Little, op. cit., vols. 4, 5.

36. W. L. Nelson, "Cost of Refineries," Oil and Gas Journal (July 29, 1974).

5

OFFSHORE ENVIRONMENTAL
EFFECTS

A lesser-known phenomenon of oil pollution is the amount and the means by which oil enters the marine environment. Although the focus of interest is a large spill near shore, biological and critical assessment must consider total inputs. The direct contribution of offshore ports to oil in the sea is very small. As part of the overall oil transport system, the impact of deepwater ports can be assessed on somewhat different bases, such as a "system" view of pollution. A second consideration, more critical from a regional perspective, is the terminal location.

The National Academy of Sciences undertook an assessment of total oil inputs and compared their results to previous estimates.[1] Among the participants of the study were authors of previous estimates of total inputs.[2] Collectively the Academy arrived at total input rates and amounts shown in Tables 5.1 and 5.2.

Approximately 35 percent of all oil is introduced through marine operations, or about 2.133 million metric tons annually. Terminal operations are estimated to account for .003 million tons--a proportion of the total which deepwater ports would not affect. Tanker accidents are also considered to have a small effect with 0.2 million tons annually, or about 3 percent of the total input. Nevertheless, of all inputs tanker accidents have the greatest potential regional impact, owing to the magnitude of one large spill.

Of all marine operations the greatest impact is from the loading and unloading of oil and associated operations of taking ballast and deballasting. Over 1 million tons are estimated to be spilled, dumped, or leaked into the marine environment through oil transfer operations. Of this total about 71 percent (0.77 million tons) comes from ships that do not use load-on-top (LOT) procedure. This procedure, which is standard on all very large crude carriers, is

TABLE 5.1

Budget of Petroleum Hydrocarbons Introduced into the Oceans
(million tons per year)

Source	Best Estimate	Input Range Probable Range		References
Natural seeps	0.6	0.2	-1.0	Wilson et al. (1973)
Offshore production	0.08	0.08	-0.15	Wilson et al. (1973)
Transportation				
LOT tankers	0.31	0.15	-0.4	Results of workshop
Non-LOT tankers	0.77	0.65	-1.0	Panel deliberations
Dry docking	0.25	0.2	-0.3	
Terminal operations	0.003	0.0015	-0.005	
Bilges bunkering	0.5	0.4	-0.7	
Tanker accidents	0.2	0.12	-0.25	
Nontanker accidents	0.1	0.02	-0.15	
Coastal refineries	0.2	0.2	-0.3	Brummage (1973)
Atmosphere	0.6	0.4	-0.8	Feuerstein (1973)
Coastal municipal wastes	0.3		--	Storrs (1973)
Coastal, nonrefining, industrial wastes	0.3		--	Storrs (1973)
Urban runoff	0.3	0.1	-0.5	Storrs (1973)/Hallhagen (1973)
River runoff*	1.6		--	Storrs (1973)
Total	6.113			Hallhagen (1973)

*Input from recreational boating assumed to be incorporated in the river runoff value.

Source: National Academy of Sciences, Ocean Affairs Board, Petroleum in the Marine Environment (Washington, D.C., 1975), p. 6.

104

designed to minimize the amount of oily water discharged from a ship when it discharges ballast before taking on a fresh crude shipment. Even though crude carriers use the less-polluting LOT system, they are not allowed by international convention to discharge oil with a visible sheen within 50 miles of the coast. If operational tanker discharges are ignored for deepwater terminal assessment, then it is primarily the threat of a major spill that figures in terminal-related oil pollution impacts.

TABLE 5.2

Comparison of Estimates for Petroleum Hydrocarbons
Annually Entering the Ocean, 1969–71
(millions of tons per annum)

	Authority		
	MIT SCEP Report (1970)	USCG Impact Statement (1973)	NAS Workshop (1973)
Marine transportation	1.13	1.72	2.133
Offshore oil production	0.20	0.12	0.080
Coastal oil refineries	0.30	--	0.200
Industrial waste	--	1.98	0.300
Municipal waste	0.45	--	0.300
Urban runoff	--	--	0.300
River runoff[a]	--	--	1.600
Subtotal	2.08	3.82	4.913
Natural seeps	?	?	0.600
Atmospheric rain-out	9.0[b]	?	~~6.113~~ 0.6
Total	11.08	?	~~6.113~~

[handwritten annotations: "0.6", "6.113", "6.113"]

[a]Input from recreational boating assumed to be incorporated in the river runoff value.

[b]Based upon assumed 10 percent return from the atmosphere.

Source: National Academy of Sciences, Ocean Affairs Board, Petroleum in the Marine Environment (Washington, D.C., 1975), p. 6.

Before turning to such an assessment, it is worth noting the relatively wide range in oil input estimates. Total pollution from marine operations has increased from the M.I.T. assessment (1970) and the Coast Guard estimate (1973). In 1971 Keith, Porricelli, and Storch estimated slightly higher inputs (2.307 million tons) from marine transportation. This latter estimate was repeated by Boesch, Hershner, and Milgram in a 1974 report to the Ford Energy Policy Project.[3] The academy estimate assumes a much lower input due to terminal operations and vessel casualties than Porricelli and Keith--0.3 compared to 0.5 million tons per year. The academy has added, however, the sources of drydocking, of which there are few facilities available for supertankers. A deepwater port terminal on the Gulf or East Coast would require expanding U.S. drydock facilities.[4]

The sources of pollution other than marine transportation have even greater variation in estimates. Some of the urban and river runoff estimated by the Academy would include oil from highway motor vehicles.

PROBABILITY OF OIL SPILLS

The primary environmental advantage of a deepwater port is the diminished probability of an oil spill. This advantage has been put forward on a number of grounds, both technological and statistical. The statistical basis depends upon accidental spill experience as compiled by the Coast Guard and other sources. The technological basis depends upon operational and other safety engineering improvements that a deepwater port may provide. Another way of looking at spill experience is to divide spills into the categories of "chronic" and "accidental." Using the Georges Bank study definition,[5] chronic spills involve causes that are presumed to be attributable to operator indifference. These are causes that could be corrected by tighter supervision and management without any real changes in technology. The other category, accidental, involves serious failure of sizable system elements. With this definition chronic spills are, as the term implies, both small and frequent; accidental spills would be larger and less frequent. In the chronic category are such occurrences as burst hoses, leaky valves, and tanker overflows. The accidental grouping would include tanker collisions, groundings, explosions, and rammings. The Georges Bank study found that chronic spills made up about 70 percent of the total number of spills and accounted for only 25 percent of the spill volume. The Georges Bank study did not focus on deepwater ports and consequently included pipelines and offshore drilling towers as leading contributors to chronic spills.

It may be easier to require better operational safety with a
deepwater port. It is also true that many of the accidental spills
could be reduced through system changes in existing ports as well
as with new offshore ports. Consequently, it is not strictly true
that new systems offer advantages only in improving the accidental
spills but not chronic spills, and that existing ports are incapable of
improving their accidental spill experience. For example, double-
bottom tankships have been estimated to provide increased effectiveness of protection between 62 to 92 percent[6]--presumably effectiveness is measured in the reduction in the number of groundings in
which tank compartments are ruptured. Double-bottom construction
is equally advantageous, whether the tanker is a VLCC accommodated
offshore or a smaller tanker using existing ports. To the extent
that double-bottom construction is the cost of increased steel to the
tankship hull, the cost may be borne equally by large and small ships.

The presumption that such improvement in accident experience
is a result of a deepwater offshore port is partially incorrect. It
would be necessary to assume that system changes of moving to an
offshore port would entail technological innovation that would not
occur otherwise.

The same study that associated deepwater ports and double-
bottom tanker construction assumed that traffic separation schemes
and in-port traffic controls would be related to reduced accident
experience at offshore ports.[7] The evidence for better traffic
management comes, however, from traffic separation in the English
Channel and a system of controls in Rotterdam. Their major improvements have developed as a result of increased traffic density,
rather than the trend toward large tankers and offshore ports.
Technological innovation may be more easily introduced in offshore
ports, but these advantages are not necessarily restricted to these
ports.[8]

For the reason that new investment and technological innovation are related, it is unfair to ignore some of the opportunities, or
even requirements, of a new system. Nevertheless, the advantages
inherent in an offshore port may be less from a strict statistical
basis if extrapolated from past experience. With respect to engineering safety to reduce accidents, it has been shown that a learning
curve can be applied to engineering systems. An accident rate reduction is evident in automobile and aircraft experience. In discussing offshore ports, the statistical data will be examined first
and engineering and design considered second.

The difference between accidental and chronic spills may be
partially the difference between small and frequent as opposed to
large and infrequent. From a biological perspective, a large spill
in a confined area is the most damaging type of spill.[9] For the

purpose of evaluating deepwater ports, it is difficult to assess
whether chronic spills would be any more or less damaging than with
existing ports. The advantages and disadvantages can be listed:

Advantages Related to Chronic Spills
1. Offshore ports are more distant from ecologically sensitive areas
and are less likely to impact these areas.
2. Offshore ports will not involve lightering at harbor entrances,
and consequently will remove one source of potential pollution.
Disadvantages Related to Chronic Spills
1. Booms and skimmers to clean up spills must be deployed "at
sea" rather than in a harbor, and consequently are less effective
owing to waves and wind.
2. Docking to a single-point mooring facility will take place in
rougher waters with no permanent pier, thus involving less environmental control over maneuvers to secure hoses and other oil transfer operations.

       To the extent that all chronic spills are a result of human error, a
better-supervised system is likely to reduce chronic spills. In
Milford Haven, an antipollution plan that required quick response and
constant surveillance was developed for the port. "The essence of
the plan is the rapid reporting of any spill by constantly patrolling
launches, shore stations, and even by the culprits themselves."
Nelson-Smith reports that this system is a least-cost solution both
to its users and to its marine life. "While no biologist could be
complacent about the situation, G. B. Crapp concluded at the end of
a three-year study of the rocky shores that no general deterioration
could be detected as a result of the first decade of operations."[10]
J. Y. Leotta and A. J. Taylor of the Coast Guard found that spills
from oil-transfer operations were reduced in the Puget Sound in the
Seattle area as a result of an intensive monitoring program. In a
pilot project, 90 percent of oil petroleum transfer operations were
monitored over a six-month period.[11] Experience alone seems to
have an effect on chronic spills, as the Milford Haven evidence
indicates that chronic spills occur more often in large ships than
smaller ones, owing to the less frequent transfers that occur on very
large crude carriers. "Dudley has observed that pollutions occur
more frequently from large crude carriers than from smaller product
tankers. He suggested that the crews of the latter are much more
experienced as a result of almost daily loading or discharging operations, whereas the larger vessels may load and discharge cargo
only once a month."[12] Nelson-Smith concluded that carelessness is
a constant cause of spillage that is compounded by language difficulties, poor communication, and inadequate supervision.

Despite these problems, Milford Haven's experience has been much better than the U.S. Coast and much better than worldwide experience. In calculating the New England coastal region spill experience, the Georges Bank study noted that their spillage rate was 50 percent higher than the Gulf Coast, but a "factor of ten higher than certain well-managed ports."[13] Spill rates for the New England region and Milford Haven are presented in Table 5.3. Mean number of spills per year per 1,000 barrels handled are given, and spill totals and percentages may be compared for Milford Haven and New England. At Milford Haven there was only one large spill, which occurred in 1967, and the other years showed total spillage of less than 10,000 gallons. These spills at Milford Haven (see Table 5.4) represent one spill for every 50 ship visits. With a throughput of 754,000 barrels per day in 1967, one 100,000 dwt tanker would be required every day for the throughput. For the purpose of a hypothetical example, 1/50 x 350 = 7 spills per year. Coast Guard data indicated 80 spills per year for the New England coastal region.

In evaluating offshore ports, it is useful to review both incidence and volume estimates. As noted for Milford Haven, it would be expected that the fraction of oil spilled as a percentage of petroleum handled is small. This fraction should decline as volume throughput increases. As large spills are infrequent, then the average yearly volume of oil spilled should be low. Offshore ports might be more conservatively estimated on the basis of spill incidence rather than volume spilled per volume handled, or even average volume spilled. For the public at large, the threat of one large spill is associated with deepwater ports.

The Georges Bank Study concluded that biologically nearshore spills were qualitatively different than offshore spills. The ecological impacts were greater and recovery times for certain nearshore species were to be measured in months and years as opposed to the days and weeks foreseen for the large offshore spill. In their conclusions the authors stated:

> We believe that the situation with respect to a large
> nearshore spill is biologically quite different from
> that associated with an offshore spill. Such a spill
> will, with high probability, come ashore while fresh.
> If the spilled material is a distillate product or a crude
> containing a substantial portion of aromatics, littoral
> and sublittoral adult as well as larval organisms will
> be subjected to toxic concentrations and substantial
> localized kills can be expected. Portions of the oil
> will be absorbed into nearshore sediments, especially
> any marshes reached, within which degradation can
> be of the order of years.[14]

TABLE 5.3

Estimates of Mean Spillage Rates as a Ratio of Production
and Transportation Activity Based on
1971 USCG Spill Reports

Source	Mean Number of Spills/Year (number per year by thousands of barrels per day)	Mean Volume Spilled (gallons per year by thousands of barrels per day)	Percent Spilled
Tankers and tank barges in re- stricted waters	.0357	386.0 1,540.0	.0025 .0100
Transfer and storage facilities	.0153	19.8* 200.0	.0001 .0010
Offshore towers	1.0100	108.0 760.0	.0007 .0050
Offshore pipelines	.1700	15.8* 160.0	.0001 .0010
Refineries	.0364	51.7* 520.0	.0003 .0030

*Upper value indicates mean as estimated directly from data;
bottom value gives probable upper estimate on actual value due to sam-
ple size errors (.68 confidence limit).

Source: M.I.T. Offshore Oil Task Group, The Georges Bank
Petroleum Study, vol. 2 (Cambridge, Mass.: M.I.T. Seagrant
Project, February 1973), p. 34.

TABLE 5.4

Quantities of Oil Spilled at Milford Haven

Year	Total Throughput (thousands of barrels per day)	Quantity Spilled Gallons	Percent Spilled
1963	234	2,600	.00008
1964	318	2,400	.00005
1965	487	9,700	.00014
1966	520	8,300	.00011
1967	507	73,000	.00095
1968	709	4,500	.00005
1969	745	4,050	.00004
Average	505	10,000	.00018

Source: M.I.T. Offshore Oil Task Group, The Georges Bank
Petroleum Study, vol. 2 (Cambridge, Mass.: M.I.T. Seagrant
Project, February 1973), p. 34.

The Georges Bank study further concluded, "Biologically we feel that all evidence, both laboratory and in the field observatories, points to the fact that the environment is considerably more vulnerable to a large nearshore spill than to a large offshore spill due to shallower water depth, higher population densities, and less mobile populations, softer sediments, and constricted waters."

Small spills offshore will be the least important biologically while large nearshore spills are the most important. In between are the chronic spills in a harbor that are, from an offshore port-assessment perspective, traded off for the threat of a large offshore spill. Chronic offshore small spills will not be examined further.

PROBABILITY ASSESSMENT

For the sake of presentation, at least two approaches to accident probabilities can be distinguished.* One approach is a statistical assessment based upon prior experience or closely related prior experience. To some extent this analysis is an extrapolation from what is known to what is not. The other approach, which is more often used for very infrequently occurring events, is based upon a systematic search of how such an event might occur, and an assessment of the likely chain of probabilities that lead to such an occurrence. In this latter approach there is a close relationship to safety engineering and decision theory. An example of the decision-theory application is the "event-tree" methodology used in the Rasmussen nuclear reactor safety study. As noted in the summary, "the risks had to be estimated rather than measured, because although there are about fifty such plants now operating, there have been no nuclear accidents to date."[15] The Rasmussen study used the event-tree methodology because the statistical data base is non-existent. Much of the analysis would depend on how failures occur or can occur in a power plant, using this knowledge to follow all paths to an accident event.

A marine example of a combination of statistical and decision theory is the presentation of the risks associated with liquefied natural gas shipping into the New York harbor.[16] In this case the analysis could not ignore that between fiscal years 1969-73 there were 20 collisions between barges and big ships in the various channels that make up the New York harbor. The analysis focused on the

*This distinction is based upon conversations with John Gardinier, Research and Development Division, U.S. Coast Guard, Washington, D.C.

36-foot draft liquefied natural gas (LNG) barge <u>Massachusetts</u>,
where barge and ship collisions were the statistical basis for probability assessment.[17] Even these 20 collisions represented only
those accidents in which 2 vessels of sufficient size were involved
that could produce a release of LNG. On an annual basis for the
entire east coast inland waters, it was found that there were 6.8 big
ship collisions per year for the period 1962-70. In the Little report,
big ships were considered those with a draft greater than 18 feet.
For large crude carriers, the deeper drafts make groundings,
rather than collisions, the greater accident risk. The threat of
groundings and rammings was dismissed in the report, owing to the
double-bottom construction and the speed with which the barge would
operate in harbor waters. With the various assumptions regarding
the operation of the LNG barge, and with a data base, it is possible
to make a probabilistic estimate of the barge being involved in an
accident. In order to estimate the probability of a LNG release, it
is necessary to turn to an analogue of the event-tree methodology.
In the Allan paper this analogue was found in the statement that,

> The probability of a spill, given that a collision has
> occurred, depends upon the structural resistance of
> the LNG ship and the circumstances of the collision.
> The circumstances specify the displacements of the
> striking ship, its velocity at the instant of impact,
> the angle made by the velocity vector with the nor-
> mal to the target ship's fore and aft line, and the
> location of the point of impact on the longitudinal
> axis of the target ship.[18]

In estimated the probability that LNG would be released, the authors
estimated that the per-voyage spill probability was 1.5×10^{-7} and
that on the basis of 53 voyages per year, the probability would be
7.7×10^{-6}, or once in every 130,000 years. Comforting as this
statistic is, LNG is released in a vapor and is easily flammable. A
fire from a burning pool of LNG at the spill site may cause severe
injury at some distance from the fire itself.[19] The authors estimate
that the danger zone is about two kilometers wide. For those who
live in the likely impacted area, yearly risk of one in 130,000 can
be compared to Rasmussen's statistics on the risk of fatality by
various causes presented in Table 5.5.

Some comparisons may be made regarding risk analysis as
it relates to an offshore port. First, risk from oil spills reflects a
risk to the coastal-zone environment rather than a direct risk to

human health.* The evaluation of oil-spill risk would then depend upon the specific degradation to the environment in which one is interested. For example, bird kills and oyster bed contamination might be considered discrete events for which an assessment can be made. It is difficult, however, to take the complex interaction of the food web and prescribe discrete events to be quantified. The question of what constitutes the discrete event still remains.

TABLE 5.5

Risk of Fatality by Various Causes

Accident Type	Total Number	Individual Chances Per Year	
Motor vehicle	55,791	1 in	4,000
Falls	17,827	1 in	10,000
Fires and hot substances	7,451	1 in	25,000
Drowning	6,181	1 in	30,000
Firearms	2,309	1 in	100,000
Air travel	1,778	1 in	100,000
Falling objects	1,271	1 in	160,000
Electrocution	1,148	1 in	160,000
Lightning	160	1 in	1,200,000
Tornadoes	91	1 in	2,500,000
Hurricanes	93	1 in	2,500,000
All accidents	111,992	1 in	1,600
Nuclear reactor accidents (100 plants)	0	1 in	300,000,000

Source: Norman C. Rasmussen, Draft Reactor Safety Study: An Assessment of Accident Risks in U.S. Commercial Nuclear Power Plants (Washington, D.C.: U.S. Atomic Energy Commission, August 1974), p. 2.

---

*There may be indirect effects insofar as toxic substances accumulate up through the food chain.

Another comparison in probability assessment is the difference in the environment in which accidents occur. For ship accidents, it is the potential magnitude of the loss of a very large crude carrier in the uncontrolled environment of the sea. Compared with nuclear reactor safety, much more is left to the whims of nature. Ships are built and men are found to sail them; they are registered under foreign flags, and owned and operated by companies from different nations. The whole tradition of the high seas leaves much more to chance than, for example, the traditions of air travel. The statistical basis for crude carrier accidents is subject to a much lesser degree of control over the environment of tanker operation than can be obtained if safety were considered more important. Some of these considerations can be included in the offshore terminal design and operation, while others require a multination approach to accident reduction.

ESTIMATE OF CRUDE OIL SPILLS
FOR AN OFFSHORE PORT

With this background on probability assessment it is possible to examine the existing data based on oil spills. Owing to the misgivings of the Georges Bank authors on their own data, this source was not considered for the analysis.[20] The other data source, often cited in the literature, is the Keith and Porricelli study conducted for the Coast Guard.[21] These authors were cited as the basis for the Russell Train paper on oil spills presented to hearings before the House of Representatives.[22] For this analysis the Keith and Porricelli data are supplemented by a similar follow-up study contracted by the Coast Guard. This second study is particularly valuable, since the authors follow the Keith and Porricelli method of analysis nearly verbatim and include an extensive appendix. Consequently, nearly four years of worldwide spill experience data are available. The Keith and Porricelli study covers 1969-70, and the J. J. Henry Company analysis covers 1971-72.[23] Because the focus of offshore terminals is the threat of a large spill, the frequency distribution of spill experience in Table 5.6 emphasizes large spill events. As noted in the table, the probability of a spill is about one in four after there is an accident, and the probability of a spill greater than 1 million gallons is about one in ten. The probability of an even larger spill of 4.4 million gallons is much less, with eight incidents in four years. On the basis of the Keith and Porricelli data alone, a frequency distribution was prepared for the Russell Train paper.[24] This frequency distribution, when plotted against the number of ships per year (or ship years), yields a reasonably straight-line plot on log-log paper.[25] The Train paper used this relationship to forecast accidents based upon the number of ships it would take for a given level of throughput. At a later point, reductions were calculated into their analysis to account for traffic separation schemes and tankship double bottoms.

TABLE 5.6

Accidents and Spill Experience, 1969-72
(worldwide data--volume in gallons)

	Years 1969-70	Years 1971-72
Number of accidents	1,416	1,587
Number of accidents in which spills occurred	266	376
Number of spills in excess of 1 million gallons	9	13
Number of spills in excess of 4.4 million gallons (29 million equals a "Torrey Canyon")	1	7
Very large crude carrier spills (150,000 dwt or greater)	11	18
Contribution to pollution incidents (percent)	(4.14%)	(4.78%)
Contribution to petroleum outflow (percent)	4,249,350 (3.13%)	711,900 (0.51%)

Sources: V. F. Keith and J. D. Porricelli, "An Analysis of Oil Outflows Due to Tanker Accidents," Prevention and Control of Oil Spills, Proceedings of a joint conference of the American Petroleum Institute, Environmental Protection Agency, and U.S. Coast Guard (Washington, D.C., March 1973); J. J. Henry Company, An Analysis of Oil Outflows Due to Tanker Accidents, prepared for the U.S. Coast Guard (Springfield, Va.: National Technical Information Service, 1973); U.S. Congress, House, Offshore Ports and Terminals, H.R. 5091 and H.R. 5898, 93rd Cong., 1st session, 1973, p. 144.

The frequency distribution presented in Table 5.7 notes that relatively few polluting accidents contribute to most of the outflow. The data in the table are for two years and are calculated directly from a Keith and Porricelli paper. Through a somewhat involved analysis, the Train paper authors arrived at an outflow tonnage and number of incidents shown in Table 5.8. Their Case I would represent the number of accidents that would occur without supertankers and Case II is their deepwater port scenario. A recapitulation of the analysis is that if approximately 40 accidents would occur without very large crude carriers, and 5 times the petroleum can be carried per ship in a very large carrier, then about 8 accidents would occur with offshore terminals. Taking some credits for technological improvements would reduce the accident experience further to 4.3 accidents, shown in Case II.

A more direct approach is to manipulate the Keith and Porricelli data and supplement it by two additional years' experience. A more conservative estimate would be produced if large crude carrier accidents are presented in terms of incidents rather than outflow, consistent with 1969-72 data. Consequently, any estimate of a large tanker being involved in a polluting incident is greater if the probability is based on the number of tankers in a fleet rather than an estimate based on the total volume of oil moved by sea.

From Table 5.6 it is now possible to make the calculations in Table 5.9. Large spill accidents (1 to 4.4 million gallons) have a probability of occurrence of about 1/3600 to 1/2300, using the 1968-72 experience and the percentage of large tankships in the total fleet. The probability would be less if outflow volume were used. With varying estimates of average tanker size between 200,000 and 300,000 deadweight tons and with differing throughput volumes, it is possible to estimate the likelihood of an offshore oil port accident. The estimate is based on exposure, whereby exposure near or at a terminal is assumed to be equal to accident exposure everywhere else the tankship is employed. This assumption will be relaxed later. The hypothetical volumes represent approximate actual total import level (both crude and product) that the United States imported from all sources to all ports in 1970 (about 2 million barrels per day) and 1974 (about 6 million). These levels of imports through offshore terminals represent likely 1985 volumes through such terminals. The probability of a large spill ranges from about 1/15200 to about 1/105300. The probability of the spill reaching shore would be less, and that portion which would reach shore would be smaller in size and toxicity than the original spill. These estimates are yearly and consequently the opportunity of a spill over the life of the facility increases. The estimate of no spills above 1 million gallons is 99.9 percent in 30 years. With 7.25 worldwide large tankship spills per

TABLE 5.7

Oil Spill Frequency Distribution, 1969-71

	Incidents			Percent of
			Oil	Total Oil
Range	Number	Percent	Outflow	Outflow
To 150 tons	139	63.47	9,695	5.75
151 to 500 tons	49	22.37	19,050	11.29
501 to 3,000 tons	22	10.05	27,120	16.07
3,000 to 14,000 tons	8	3.65	63,690	37.74
Greater than 14,000 tons	1	0.46	49,200	29.15
Total	219	100.00	168,755	100.00

Source: Calculated from J. D. Porricelli, V. F. Keith, and R. L. Storch, "Tankers and the Ecology," Transactions of the Society of Naval Architects and Marine Engineers 79 (1971) presented in Attachment B, Statement of Russell E. Train, Special Joint Subcommittee on Deepwater Port Legislation, U.S. Congress, Senate, Deepwater Port Act of 1973, S.1751 and S.2232, Serial 93-59, 93rd Cong., 1st session, 1973.

TABLE 5.8

Comparative Tanker Casualties over 20 Years

	Number of Incidents		Number of Tons Spilled	
Range of Spills	Case I	Case II	Case I	Case II
1 to 150	24.00	3.00	1,680.0	186.0
151 to 500	8.50	0.65	3,306.5	250.3
501 to 3,000	3.80	0.44	4,674.0	514.8
3,000 to 14,000	1.40	0.21	11,144.0	1,577.1
14,000 +	0.17	--	8,364.0	--
Total	37.87	4.30	29,168.5	2,528.2

Notes: Assumptions: Throughput 2 million barrels per day in both cases. Case I represents oil transported to conventional ports in tankers averaging 50,000 dwt. Case II represents oil transported to offshore terminals in supertankers averaging 250,000 dwt--transshipment to shore via pipeline.

Source: Attachment A, Statement of Russell E. Train, Special Joint Subcommittee on Deepwater Port Legislation, U.S. Congress, Senate, Deepwater Port Act of 1973, S.1751 and S.2232, Serial 93-39, 93rd Cong., 1st session, 1973, p. 87.

TABLE 5.9

Probability Estimates of Large Crude Carrier Spills

Spill Data	Spills/Year 161	1 Million Gallon Spill/Year 5.5[a]	4.4 Million Gallon Spill/Year 2[a]
Large crude carrier spill data and estimates	7.25	4.3×10^{-4}	2.8×10^{-4}

Throughput/Tankship Size
(million barrels per day/thousand deadweight tons)

Large crude carrier	2 MM b/d 200 dwt/300 dwt		6 MM b/d 200 dwt/300 dwt	
Exposure days to accidents[b] (near coast or terminal)	1,460	973	4,380	2,919
Percent of exposure days: all tankships worldwide (1969-72)	5.1%	3.4%	15.4%	10.3%
Large crude carrier spills (coastal zone)	0.37	0.25	1.12	0.75
Probability of spill of 1 million gal. (coastal zone)	2.2×10^{-5}	1.5×10^{-5}	6.6×10^{-5}	4.4×10^{-5}
Probability of spill of 4.4 million gal. (coastal zone)	1.4×10^{-5}	9.5×10^{-4}	4.3×10^{-5}	2.9×10^{-5}

[a]Based upon the number of tankships in the world fleet during 1969-72. Excludes the 10,000 dwt vessels for spills greater than 4.4 million gallons.

[b]Based upon two days at terminal and one day for inbound and outbound, with the number of tankships of the given size.

Source: Table 5.6.

year, and an exposure of 3.4 percent to 15.4 percent per year, then
a 30-year spill frequency ranges from 7 accidents to 33 accidents.
Large spills, irrespective of source, are slightly more frequent
(7.5 per year) and the upper bound of accidents may be 35 accidents.

Thus far it has been assumed that accidents are equally likely
to occur every day of the year. In fact, about 20 percent of the
spills occur at sea and about one-quarter occur along coastal areas.
The majority of accidents, the remaining 55 percent, occur in areas
where the threat to the environment is considerable. The four-year
locational distribution of accidents (Table 5.10) shows that offshore
oil ports are advantageous to the extent that harbors are avoided altogether. If the offshore terminals are located 10 to 20 miles at
sea, all harbor accidents and some coastal accidents are avoidable.
Fairways would exist for large tank ships as entranceways to the
monobuoy. Such "entrance" accidents would still occur and there
is still the potential for "pier-type" accidents. Assuming that all
voyages have an equal likelihood of an accident, and that sea accidents and harbor accidents may be ignored for assessment of deepwater ports, then a hypothetical exposure could be calculated to
compare with the previous table, which assumed three days' exposure out of the year. With 10 percent of the world's seaborne oil
destined for North America, the calculation of exposure for Table
5.9 would be .1 x 1/2 (.26 coastal + .16 entrance + .16 pier) = 2.9
percent of worldwide accidents. The actual exposure is considerably less, given the greater petroleum handling activity of Western
European, Persian Gulf, and Japanese ports. The 2.9 percent
probability with a 7.25 worldwide accident experience yields 0.21
accidents per year.

On the basis of spill volume, the greatest single loss of oil is
due to structural failure at sea, with 31 percent of all oil spills.
In heavy weather it is better to dump the oil then to risk losing the
ship, and there is some evidence that dumping occurs frequently.[26]
The 1969-72 analyses on spill data found a correlation between age
of ship and the frequency of structural failures.[27] The five total
losses in 1971-72 were to ships with an average age of 18 years.[28]
The next two leading causes of accidents are groundings and collisions with each having about 21 percent of the total outflow. Owing
to the deeper drafts, large tankships are particularly susceptible
to groundings. The coastal area and entrances are understandably
the scene of most groundings. Collisions occur frequently in
harbors and harbor entrances, but the serious collisions are in
coastal areas.

TABLE 5.10

Distribution of 642 Spills by Location

Year	Coastal	Entrance	Harbor	Pier	Sea	Unknown	Total
1969–70	60 (23)	59 (22)	45 (17)	43 (16)	52 (20)	7 (2)	266 (100)
1971–72	109 (29)	44 (12)	95 (25)	57 (15)	68 (18)	3 (1)	376 (100)
Percent of total	(26)	(16)	(22)	(16)	(19)	(1)	(100)

Note: Figures in parentheses represent percentages.
Sources: V. F. Keith and J. D. Porricelli, "An Analysis of Oil Outflows Due to Tanker Accidents," Prevention and Control of Oil Spills, Proceedings of a joint conference of the Petroleum Institute, Environmental Protection Agency, and U.S. Coast Guard (Washington, D.C., March 1973); J. J. Henry Company, An Analysis of Oil Outflows Due to Tanker Accidents, prepared for the U.S. Coast Guard (Springfield, Va.: National Technical Information Service, 1973).

TABLE 5.11

Percentage Distribution of Total 869,774 Ton Outflow by Cause, Location, and Number

(1968–72)

Type of Casualty	Coastal	Entrance	Harbor	Pier	Sea	Unknown	Total
Breakdown	<1%	<1%	<1%	<1%	2(1)%	<1%	2%
Collision	18(65)	1(40)	1(54)	1	1	<1	21
Explosion	2(8)	0	1	2(18)	6(14)	<1	11
Fire	<1	<1	<1	<1	<1	<1	1
Grounding	7(71)	10(51)	4(47)	0	0	<1	21
Ramming	0	1	1	1	1	<1	1
Structural failure	5(7)	<1	<1	<1	31(79)	<1	37
Capsizing and other	2(5)	<1	<1	<1	4(4)	0	6

Note: Number of incidents in parentheses.

Source: V. F. Keith and J. D. Porricelli, "An Analysis of Oil Outflows Due to Tanker Accidents," Prevention and Control of Oil Spills, Proceedings of a joint conference of the American Petroleum Institute, Environmental Protection Agency, and U.S. Coast Guard (Washington, D.C., March 1973); J. J. Henry Company, An Analysis of Oil Outflows Due to Tanker Accidents, prepared for the U.S. Coast Guard (Springfield, Va.: National Technical Information Service, 1973).

SPILL FREQUENCY: LOOP AND SEADOCK

Both projects estimated the likelihood of accidents using a somewhat similar, but more thorough, analysis. Several differences stand out in these project estimates. For example, for small spills U.S. Coast Guard data were used rather than worldwide experience. It is more likely that such small spills will go unreported overseas than in U.S. waters. These project estimates also used only 1971-72 data as a base for larger ship spills (over 300,000 dwt) and consequently had a higher proportion of very large spills than if four years of worldwide data were used.

Despite these differences, the frequencies of spills were similar. SEADOCK arrived at 0.14 spills per year from a volume of 4 million barrels per day. The LOOP project arrived at 0.21 spills per year from 2 million barrels per day.[29] The SEADOCK project took several accident-reduction credits based upon traffic-density exposure rates, room for maneuverability, and improved regulations and communications regarding tank ship operations. Although such risk-reduction factors are somewhat arbitrary, they are reasonable when applied to the spill data base. SEADOCK arrived at a per vessel spill probability and then applied the frequency to the tankship exposure level expected in order to arrive at an overall spill frequency.

Both projects based exposure on a mix of different-size vessels that would arrive at each offshore port. Unlike the earlier discussion, such exposure includes small vessels for transshipment and medium-sized tankships, as well as large carriers. Such a distribution of ships increases the total number of vessels calling on the port and will increase the expected frequency of spills.

Both SEADOCK and LOOP fit spill-frequency data to log normal curve to estimate spills of various magnitudes. Using such curves to estimate the probability of a spill will increase the estimate of a large spill, owing to the cumulative frequency of various-size spill estimates. Such estimates of probability shown in Table 5.9 are better than the earlier appraisal where the probability of no spill above 1 million gallons (about 24,000 barrels) was 99.7 percent.

Due to the use of a probability distribution curve to estimate spills, both projects made a determination of when the curve ceased to be valid. This was called the maximum credible spill. This term indicates where mathematical probability from the curve was at variance with the ability to conceive of how an accident can happen over a certain size. Both projects chose 120,000 barrels as the maximum credible spill. This size spill would constitute most of the oil held in a VLCC wing tank (145,000 barrels). Whether or not such a size spill is indeed the credible limit remains speculative.

From Table 5.12 it can be seen that the frequency of spills and expectation of spills over 30 years (about 4 per year for SEADOCK) are comparable to earlier estimates. These data represent tank-ship spills only and do not include other possible causes of accidents, such as pipeline failures, hose breaks at the terminal, or accidents at the tank farm or salt domes. As tankship accidents represent the more serious large event, only these accidents are considered here. They were included, however, in the project application.

There is some variance regarding the potential for a very large crude carrier accident, however, as LOOP expects a 96.3 percent probability of a 100,000-barrel accident will not occur and SEADOCK estimates a 98.5 percent probability. Using LOOP data, there is about a 50 percent probability that sometime over 30 years there will be an accident greater than 20,000 barrels.

The value in such estimates is clearly not in the ability to predict an accident, but whether more can be done to prevent an accident. The numbers only indicate that spill-prevention procedures are essential and central to these projects. A second consideration is where to emphasize spill prevention and what alternatives may be available in siting ports.

Whatever risks are involved in deepwater ports, it is apparent that spill risks are greater elsewhere than in a well-managed port facility. Traffic density is the only major factor contributing to offshore spills that is not present in other tankship operations. Traffic density is the one area where offshore ports have the advantage over existing ports, while the greater potential for poor weather conditions represents the major disadvantage in offshore ports.

PREVENTION OF OIL SPILLS

Although spill cleanup procedures and techniques are constantly improving, they are no substitute for prevention, particularly off-shore in higher seas. Some of the preventive measures can be in-corporated into the design and operation of the port, while others are based on extending the operation of the terminal to control over the operation of the large crude carriers. Congress emphasized the safety and oil spill prevention measures in passing the Deepwater Port Act of 1974. Their emphasis has been shown by licensing the deepwater port operator and making the grant of such a license contingent upon numerous reviews and interagency coordination de-cisions. The license requirement puts the burden of proof squarely on the licensee. Authority for issuance of the license ultimately rests with the secretary of the department in which the Coast Guard is operating. This phrase indicates the intent of Congress with

TABLE 5.12

Accident Frequency and Probability: SEADOCK and LOOP
(2 million barrels per day at each port)

Spill Class (barrels)	Annual Frequency		Chance of No Spills in 30 Years		Expectation of Spills in 30 Years*	
	LOOP	SEADOCK	LOOP	SEADOCK	LOOP	SEADOCK
Less than 1,000	.0480	.0593	22.9%	--		1.78
1,000–20,000	.1359	.0753	1.25	9.6%		2.25
20,000–100,000	.0228	.0054	49.6	85.0		0.16
>100,000	.0013	.0004	96.3	98.8		0.03
Total	.2080	.1404				4.22

*Based upon a probability density curve.

Sources: LOOP, Inc., Application for License, 22 vols. (Washington, D.C.: U.S. Coast Guard, 1975); SEADOCK, Inc., Application for License, 5 vols. (Washington, D.C.: U.S. Coast Guard, 1975).

respect to offshore port management, without adjudicating within which federal agency (Interior, Transportation, or Environmental Protection) the authority shall reside. The Nixon administration had originally intended to place the function in Interior, although a few congressmen were outspoken that it is better placed in Transportation, where it is now located. By placing the Coast Guard in authority, Congress has chosen the agency that can prescribe navigation rules, board ships, and assume some of the police functions that may be needed to prevent accidents.

PROCEDURAL REGULATION

The procedural regulations called for in the Deepwater Port Act include: (1) site selection involving coordination with Interior and the National Oceanic and Atmospheric Administration; and (2) submission of offshore terminal plans and their publication in the Federal Register. The plans shall include "a description of procedures to be used in constructing, operating and maintaining, the deepwater port including system of oil spill prevention, containment and cleanup."[30] The secretary of the department in which the Coast Guard is operating (Transportation) must coordinate with the other federal agencies, take their comments into account, and an environmental impact statement must be prepared, and subsequent public hearings must be held. The secretary shall approve or deny the application within 90 days after the last public hearing. In Section 6 of the act, the environmental review criteria are stated that follow and reflect the intent of the National Environmental Policy Act of 1969, as it applies to deepwater ports.

Another procedural step that may have little to do with oil-spill prevention, but represents a potent lever to decisions, is the requirement that the "Secretary shall not issue a license without the approval of the Governor of each adjacent coastal state."[31] The meaning of "adjacent coastal state" provoked some discussions in the hearings. As the act reads, the Administrator of the National Oceanic and Atmospheric Administration (NOAA) "shall . . . designate as an 'adjacent coastal state' any coastal state as to which there is substantial risk of serious damage, because of such factors as prevailing winds and currents, to its coastal environment as a result of oil spill incidents that originate from the proposed deepwater port or from any vessel located within the safety zone around such deepwater port."[32]

In making his determination of "substantial risk" the administrator would have to consider that the Georges Bank study reviewed the spreading histories of five oil spills and found that a 1 million gallon spill could spread over one square mile in two days.[33] Further hypothetical calculation under a condition of a .1 southwest current showed that a 10 million gallon spill launched in summer 1 nautical mile offshore from Machias Bay, Maine, still had a 10 percent probability of hitting a 1.8 nautical mile length of shore 49 miles south of the launch point.[34] The overall probability was estimated at 5 percent that a 1 million gallon spill would deposit 30,000 to 50,000 gallons some distance along the coast from the launch point of the spill.[35] The probability profile of a spill according to the Georges Bank study showed that the bulk of oil is distributed around the launch point with one tail reaching along the coast of the prevailing wind and current.

The NOAA administrator would have to consider the site of each prospective port, and possibly designate one additional "adjacent coastal state" in the path of prevailing winds and current.[36] States with limited coastlines, such as New Hampshire, Rhode Island, Connecticut, New York, Delaware, and Maryland, may have to consider deepwater port decisions as joint decisions with at least one other sister state. Maine, Louisiana, and Texas, with extensive coastlines, should be less affected by such determination of adjacent coastal state.

The SEADOCK project developed a model similar to the Georges Bank study to evaluate the spreading pattern of large oil spills. The initial intent of the model was to determine the probability of an oil spill reaching shore without clean up efforts. The study found a 10 percent probability of oil-slick landfall in the area west of Freeport, Texas. Their assessment of reasonable limits of impact area extends from Corpus Christi to Port Arthur.[37] Based upon this assessment, SEADOCK stated that adjacent coastal state status ought to be confined to Texas.[38]

Florida has already requested adjacent coastal state status, presumably for the LOOP project.[39] In undertaking their risk analysis the LOOP project discussed accident potential in the straits of Florida. The discussion tended to show that oil-spill risk depends more on the amount of oil refined on the Gulf Coast and shipped to the East Coast, then the use of the Florida straits for crude oil shipped from Africa and the Persian Gulf. The problem of coastal shipping accidents is somewhat a general issue of responsibility rather than an issue in impact assessment of a deepwater port. The LOOP project expects that most crude oil will be shipped through the more dangerous but shorter Yucatan and Old Bahama passage, which will not affect Florida.

The question of adjacent coastal state appears to depend on the definition of how much petroleum transport activity can be attributed to a deepwater port. Given that the definition limits impact

to oil-spill risks in the vicinity of the monobuoys, then an oil slick
spreading model can be used to determine which areas are affected.

A considerable amount of time was taken during the hearings
in discussion over whether a governor would have veto power over a
deepwater port. Congress has decided in favor of such a veto power
and has extended this power to contiguous states, which the NOAA
administrator might designate. The administration position expressed by John Love, former governor of Colorado and director of
the Energy Policy Office, stated that neither "Federal preemption
nor State veto" shall exist. The state position was expressed by
Senator Johnston of Louisiana, who was unconvinced of John Love's
assurances that land-use planning and environmental laws would
apply and "for all practical purposes, the State is going to decide."

> Senator Johnston: If the Senator would yield, I have
> heard this answer so well stated by Governor Love
> that he recommends no Federal preemption, but no
> state veto with the right of consultation. I would
> submit that if you give the Federal Government the
> right to grant the license and you do not give the
> State the right to veto, you have preempted the
> field. You have given the Federal Government the
> right to build the Superport whether the State wants
> it or not. . . .[40]

Giving the states the veto power, as the act has, will maintain
interest in the environmental safeguards related to spill prevention
through the state's right to review, reject, or approve the application for a license. The legal status by which a state acquires the
right to veto is through designation. This designation is acquired
as a matter of right by the state with the landward pipeline connection or any state within 15 miles of the proposed deepwater port.
Any additional designations depend on the environmental criteria
of the NOAA Administrator.[41]

Congress made the Coast Guard responsible for development
of criteria for environmental protection procedures. The Coast
Guard has begun to develop such regulations. The initial requirements are much less informative than the SEADOCK and LOOP
applications.[42] The applications contain specific criteria for port
shut down and operational procedures in case of adverse weather or
other dangerous situations. For example, the SEADOCK application
contains criteria on: shutdown of oil transfer, conditions under
which tankships may leave mooring, mooring prohibition situations,
and complete shutdown and evacuation. In discussing port operations the SEADOCK application makes individual responsibilities of

the personnel quite clear. Moreover, both LOOP and SEADOCK
studied in depth such questions as sea floor keel clearance, storm
conditions, and simulation of stress conditions at the Netherlands
Ship Model Basin.[43]

Congress did not and could not specify these operational and
design considerations. Congress did specify criminal penalties,
civil penalties, and authorized civil-suit action by individuals.
These provisions are in addition to a special environmental fund
that shall be used on a cleanup first and settle-up later basis. The
penalty for not reporting an oil spill is $10,000 and the liability for
cleanup is $20 million to the vessel owner or operator, and $100
million to the port licensee, depending upon who is in control at the
time of the spill. These maximum penalties are "without regard to
fault" and if "gross negligence or willful misconduct" is found, the
vessel operator or owner, or the licensee may be liable for the
full costs of cleanup.

Congress wisely set up a separate fund for a permanent level
of $100 million to be paid for by a 2 cents per barrel charge from
the oil throughput. Such a fund would be used for cleanup until
liability is fixed. A citizen could sue the fund for damages rather
than recover the damages from the guilty parties directly. The fund
represents a ready source for cleanup and recovery of damage,
while the liability penalties represent a deterrent to careless oil
transfer. Fault is found, but it does not detract from rapid response
to spill cleanup.

Although offshore terminals are included in the EPA definition
of "best available technology," and the Coast Guard will apply
stringent operating procedures, there is still some limit to control
over vessel operation and design. To a great extent, offshore port
operation is limited by the worldwide nature of tankship construction and operation. International treaty, rather than offshore port-
licensing procedure, is the instrument to safer operation of the
vessels. As Nelson-Smith summarizes the Torrey Canyon disaster,
it "was the ultimate demonstration of the combined effects of this
lack of maneuverability, faulty crew training and communication,
and inadequate navigational aids."[44] The offshore port licensee has
no control over crude carriers built with single rather than double
screws (maneuverability) for the failure to keep the chart room
stocked or the lack of Decca Navigator to improve knowledge of
position. As these factors contributed to the Torrey Canyon spill,
the potential for accidents still exists. Added to these factors are
insufficient lights for night, poor training, too few tank compartments to avoid multiple ruptures, and the inability to quickly shift
oil from a ruptured tank to other tanks.

The Coast Guard has begun to set requirements on tankships
pursuant to Congressional mandate under the Ports and Waterways
Safety Act of 1972. The proposed rules are primarily noted for the
requirement of segregated ballast. U.S. tankers, whether in domestic or foreign trade, and foreign-flag tankers entering U.S.
waters must, if newly built, have segregated ballast. The requirement does not apply to existing tankships.[45] Generally, Coast
Guard requirements follow the 1973 International Marine Consultive
Organization (IMCO) Conference on Marine Pollution. These international treaty provisions will be examined presently.

TECHNICAL IMPROVEMENT AND INTERNATIONAL
LAW: DOUBLE BOTTOMS

The method by which the additional design features are introduced is through international treaty, including Law of the Sea
conferences and conferences of the Intergovernmental Maritime
Consultive Organization. The complications of maritime law are
recounted by Nelson-Smith about the Torrey Canyon: "She was an
American-owned tanker flying the Liberian flag and operated by an
Italian crew, on charter to the British Petroleum Company whose
oil she was carrying to Milford Haven, when she struck a reef which
is technically in international waters. The resulting spill severely
polluted both British and French shores." Not only are the issues
international, but there has been some question as to which conference proceedings to submit these issues to. For example, if the
United States wanted to require double bottoms (two layers of steel
in the hull rather than one) on the Alaskan oil trade to the West
Coast, it could be done.[46] The Coast Guard has not proposed
double bottoms[47] and such a requirement was rejected by the IMCO
Conference on marine pollution.[48] The Law of the Sea Conference
was considered by IMCO as the appropriate arena to determine the
right of the United States or any other nation to require double bottoms on another nation's vessels entering her ports. The legal
basis for unilateral action would be determined by the Law of the
Sea. Although the IMCO Conference rejected double bottoms and
deferred "jurisdictional" disputes to the Law of the Sea, they did
require more stringent pollution measures (Table 5.13). Nevertheless, the offshore port nation can only inspect and detain foreign-
flag vessels and it cannot prosecute unless the vessel is in its
jurisdiction. Jurisdiction is defined by flag of registry. Jurisdiction is extended by way of the Law of the Sea. As a consequence,
IMCO left prosecution of violations of its own treaty provisions to

TABLE 5.13

International Conference on Marine Pollution, 1973: Portions Applicable
to U.S. Deepwater Ports

Regulation	Use	Reference
Oil prevention certificate for each tanker; requires survey of new ships prior to service and periodic survey of existing fleet.	Maintain a licensing provision to assist operation of a safe tankship fleet; encourages nations to join IMCO and abide by its rules.	Regulations 5 and 6
Control of discharge of oil. Prohibits discharge within 50 nautical miles of land; beyond 50 miles prohibits discharge in excess of 1/15,000 of cargo for existing ships and 1/30,000 for new ships. Discharge must be enroute at a rate not in excess of 60 liters per nautical mile.	Provides protection against operation discharges of oil which could affect the coastal zone; provides a criterion which can be monitored by Coast Guard: Facts may be investigated "whenever visible traces of oil are observed on or below the surface of the water."	Chapter 2, Regulation 9. Control of Discharge of Oil
Every new oil tanker of 70,000 tons deadweight and above shall be provided with segregated ballast tanks.	Provides for clean ballast whereby the likelihood of oil/water mixtures in tanks during ballast voyages is much reduced.	Regulation 13
Dirty ballast residue and tank cleaning residue transferred to slop tanks and effluent discharge not to exceed Regulation 9 (above). Device fitted on board to monitor oil discharge and Oil Record Book required, and oil/water interface detectors. Requires oil/water separator to reduce oil content to 100 ppm, or filter system to reduce to 15 ppm. Sludge tanks needed for residue.	Provides equipment provisions to meet effluent discharge requirements for both new and existing vessels. Requires the method of "load on top."	Retention of oil on board, Regulation 15 Oil discharge control, Regulations 16 and 17
In every oil tanker a discharge manifold for connection to reception facilities for the discharge of dirty ballast water or oil contaminated water shall be located on the open deck.	Provides for visible above waterline discharge and controlled discharge in port or at a terminal.	Regulation 18
Cargo tanks of oil tankers shall be of such size and arrangement that the hypothetical oil outflow doesn't exceed 40,000 cubic meters. Formulae for calculating hypothetical oil outflow and other tank size criteria are provided.	Limits tank sizes in order to reduce potential oil outflow from an accident in which the damage can be confined to ruptured tanks.	Regulations 22, 23, and 24

Note: PPM equals parts per million.

Source: Inter-Governmental Maritime Consultative Organization, Final Act of the International Conference on Marine Pollution, 1973 (London, November 1973).

the state which is the flag of registry. In this case, a pollution incident occurring on the high seas to an American-owned tanker flying the Liberian flag would be prosecuted by Liberia. The offshore port licensee would have the power to detain the vessel as it entered the port safety zone "until it can sail without presenting an unreasonable threat to the marine environment." By deferring to the Law of the Sea conference in Resolution 23 and elsewhere, the IMCO Conference did not attempt to define these legal questions.

On the subject of double bottoms, the American oil companies have presented a technical argument against double bottoms.[49] Opposition to the requirement of double bottoms is not limited to other nations, as Russell Train's statement implies: "I think I would say generally that the U.S. found very little support amongst the other countries at the conference for the concept of double bottoms for which we were pushing."[50] This lack of support extends to American oil companies and shipping interests generally. The Congressional Office of Technology Assessment has made a favorable review of double bottoms,[51] but the Coast Guard has not proposed double bottoms even for vessels in domestic trade.[52]

The double bottoms example is useful because it shows how difficult it is to legislate and enforce pollution conventions. Control of worldwide pollution is logically placed in an international forum, such as IMCO. Nonetheless, adjacent coastal states are penalized in light of their own limited powers to enforce the conditions of oil transfer.

U.S. interests appear to be defined in terms of status as a maritime nation. U.S. interest and commerce outweigh perceived environmental benefit from nations regulating oil discharge off their coast but in international waters. Apparently, the risks of being regulated outweigh the benefits of being a regulator.[53]

VLCC SAFETY FEATURES

In an evaluation of the U.S. tanker construction program, the Maritime Administration (MARAD) considered some of the technical improvements to tankships.[54] These improvements, as shown in Table 5.14, represent those features that are not part of either the U.S. or other tankship construction programs. Of the features listed, the Maritime Administration Construction Program does include double bottom protection. In addition to the safety improvements listed in the table, Noel Mostert would add adequate auxiliary power, including electric power, which includes spare boilers and spare evaporator equipment for making fresh boiler water. Mostert has commented extensively on the lack of redundant engineering

TABLE 5.14

Estimated Oil Outflow Reduction and Cost of Vessel Improvement
(yearly estimated reduction in cubic meters in first two lines)[a]

	Bow Thruster	Inert Gas System	Controllable Pitch Propeller	Twin Screw	Reduce Tank Size by 1/2	Double Bottom	Segregated[c] Ballast
VLCC 225[b]	3.1	57	9.1	21.4	50	131–155	45
VLCC 265[b]	3.3	82	10.5	26.8	60	131–155	53
Incremental cost[d]	4%	1%	3%	8%	2%	18%	4–9%

[a]Cubic meter is equal to approximately 264 gallons of crude oil.
[b]In thousands of deadweight tons.
[c]Segregated ballast increased up to 45 percent of full load displacement.
[d]Estimated increase in construction cost to a design which now meets IMCO requirements on oil outflow limitations.

Note: All outflow reduction is based on accident probability except increased segregated ballast.

Source: U.S. Department of Commerce, Maritime Administration, "Tanker Construction Program," Draft Environmental Impact Statement, vol. I, EIS 730392D (Washington, D.C., undated).

systems in VLCC construction and has contrasted this with the care
taken with older-generation ship construction. The author cites
such examples as the inability to make steam flash boilers, and
power failures that lead to total blackout.[55]

TABLE 5.15

Ranking of Oil Pollution Reduction Features

	According Impact on Outflow Reduction Probability	According to Cost Effectiveness
1. Double bottoms	1	3 or 4
2. 45% Segregated ballast	2	2
3. Reduce tank size 50%	3	1
4. Twin screws	4	5
5. Controllable pitch propellers	5	3 or 4
6. Bow thrusters	6	6

Notes: The following procedures and systems are considered
standard on new properly designed tankships of VLCC class: Load
on top, segregated ballast (IMCO), inert gas system, electronic
collision-avoidance systems, fixed tank cleaning equipment, and
oily water separators.

Cost effectiveness is simply the estimated reduction in pollution divided by the incremental cost.

Source: U.S. Department of Commerce, Maritime Administration, "Tanker Construction Program," Draft Environmental
Impact Statement, vol. I, EIS 730392D (Washington, D.C., undated).

In commenting on these safety features, it is the ability to
turn to alternate systems in case of emergency that cannot be evaluated by a checklist. Such safety-design features would require a
more complex evaluation to assess their added value. As with all
safety considerations, the benefits are based upon the number of
accidents that are avoided. For most of this chapter, such accident
reduction is considered in terms of probability.

The benefit calculation in Table 5.14 is the indirect assessment of one author's evaluation of the accident-reduction potential
of each safety consideration: twin screws, double bottoms, con-

trollable pitch propellers. Moreover, a very thorough accident experience would have to be undertaken to confirm this benefit assessment. Another method of assessment is to carefully describe what
each safety feature does, and illustrate the situations in which these
additional precautions are useful. A still third comparison is to
indicate a standard of performance and evaluate whether a VLCC
meets the requirement. A recent review of double bottoms indicates
that added cost of this protection is much less than 18 percent and
the actual range is from 3 to 5 percent higher cost.[56]

Mostert cites several instances that represent the latter two
bases of comparison. For example, very large crude carriers are
still being built with one very high pressure boiler, when two or
more have been the norm.[57] Another example cited is the Gulf Oil
LUDWIG 326,000 ton ships provided with twin screws and rudders
that could come to a crash stop in two miles, about the same distance it takes a 50,000 ton vessel.[58] Most supertankers with a
single screw take three miles and 20 minutes to come to a full stop.
Twin screws and controllable pitch propellers are important to
maneuverability, but there is no standard of performance for a
VLCC, nor are accidents solely due to maneuverability. During
1971-72, two polluting accidents to ships over 100,000 dwt were
identified as having maneuverability as a factor.[59] Although most
accidents are due to human error, and even though many operational changes could be made, certain improvements can only be
made through design.

The VLCC was built for economy, with a write-off life of
ten years. The competitive-advantage argument was noted as one
reason for the resistance to double bottoms at the IMCO Conference.
The United States could set the lead in design safety rather than turn
out ships that merely meet IMCO standards.

Turning back to Tables 5.14 and 5.15, the benefit assessment
is highly speculative. The environmental impact statement on the
MARAD program failed to ask certain crucial questions, and therefore, such comparisons are not in the proper context. Design features must be considered in a variety of operational circumstances,
taking into account both well and poorly managed ships. Technical
assessment should distinguish between pollution design features for
improving day to day operations and those design features for accident reduction.[60] Above all, the IMCO standard should be improved
upon rather than merely accepted.

CONCLUSIONS: EAST COAST AND GULF COAST

The refined distillates are considered more toxic than crude
oil, but physical smothering is more likely with crude oil or ship

bunker oil.[61] Offshore spills are less damaging than nearshore spills, except to the extent that there is a potential of a spill of much larger size.

A deepwater port would reduce the likelihood of collisions, owing to the reduction in the ship-traffic density. These advantages of an offshore port are lessened if much of the incoming foreign crude oil is transshipped in barges from the offshore port to existing ports. In case of transshipment, the only advantage of a deepwater terminal is in the operational and safety-design advantages of the port itself. This technological advantage may be considerable, owing to lightering operations that now occur.

If a deepwater crude oil port is not built, then it is more likely that East Coast ports will receive petroleum products. Products are more toxic and the size of the product tanker can rise to the limit of East Coast draft accommodation.

In New England, an offshore port sited in Maine would probably induce transshipment of crude southward to the Middle Atlantic states. There would be more traffic near the terminal, but the impact of crude carriers near the coast may not be much different than having the terminal in Canada. If the port were located in a natural deepwater harbor, the immediate harbor area would be impacted by chronic small spills and the environmental damage would be greater in case of a large spill.

In the Middle Atlantic states, an offshore port located near New York harbor or Delaware Bay would provide an incentive to greater refinery expansion. Regardless of refinery decisions, more crude oil and less refined oil would be imported. This particular environmental effect may be considered positive.

If the offshore port used pipelines direct to refineries, the threat of a spill would be less than with a system of transshipment barges. An offshore crude oil port with pipelines to refineries is preferable to large product carriers using existing ports, all other things being equal.

The deepwater port licensee and the Coast Guard have limited ability to control the operation of very large crude carriers. There may be an advantage, however, in operating a well-run offshore port and maintaining some control in the port area, rather than risk an even less-controlled situation.

Overall, a deepwater crude oil port will substitute crude oil for products and increase total petroleum movement to the extent that refinery capacity is increased. Under this circumstance, less oil would come from the Gulf and more would arrive from overseas. This shift will affect the regional oil-spill impact, but should not affect total oil inputs into the sea. There may be some slight overall improvement in inputs through the reduction in petroleum cross-hauling. By and large the potential pollution would be transferred from the Gulf Coast to the East Coast.

From a purely biological point of view whereby any oil inputs to the sea should be reduced, offshore oil ports represent one principal advantage in providing an opportunity to set up improved systems for oil transfer. This opportunity has the momentum of the economic incentive for offshore construction.

The SEADOCK and LOOP projects increase the potential for a crude oil spill in the immediate area of the port. Otherwise, oil-spill impacts primarily depend upon the level of imports. These two projects, if carefully designed, constructed, and operated, represent a step forward in the shipping and handling of oil. Alternatives to offshore ports would offer no greater safety. The use of existing ports or extensive transshipment only increases the probability of accidents.

NOTES

1. National Academy of Sciences, Ocean Affairs Board, Petroleum in the Marine Environment (Washington, D.C., 1975), Chapter I.

2. J. D. Porricelli, V. F. Keith, and R. L. Storch, "Tankers and the Ecology," Transactions of the Society of Naval Architects and Marine Engineers 79 (1971).

3. Donald F. Boesch, Carl Hershner, and Jerome H. Milgram, Oil Spills and the Marine Environment (Cambridge, Mass.: Ballinger, 1974).

4. U.S. Department of Commerce, Maritime Administration, "Tanker Construction Program," Draft Environmental Impact Statement, vol. I (Washington, D.C., undated).

5. M.I.T. Offshore Oil Task Group, The Georges Bank Petroleum Study, vol. 2 (Cambridge, Mass.: M.I.T. Seagrant Project, February 1973), p. 18.

6. Attachment A, "Tanker Oil Spill Probabilities," appended to the statement of Russell E. Train, U.S. Congress, House, Offshore Ports and Terminals, H.R. 5091 and H.R. 5898, 93rd Cong., 1st session, 1973, p. 146.

7. Ibid., pp. 143-53.

8. As an example see U.S. Coast Guard, "New York Vessel Traffic System," Draft Environmental Impact Statement (New York, 1974).

9. National Academy of Sciences, Petroleum in the Marine Environment, p. 98.

10. A. Nelson-Smith, Oil Pollution and Marine Ecology (New York: Plenum Press, 1973), pp. 174-75; G. B. Crapp, "Monitoring the Rocky Shore," Ecological Effects of Oil Pollution on Littoral Communities (London: Institute of Petroleum, 1971), pp. 102-03.

11. J. V. Leotta and A. J. Taylor, "Coast Guard Transfer Monitoring Program," Prevention of Oil Spills: Proceedings of Joint Conference (Washington, D.C.: American Petroleum Institute, 1973).

12. Nelson-Smith, op. cit., p. 64; the Milford Haven terminal operator agrees with the assessment of large versus small tanker-spill experience. The M.I.T. Offshore Oil Task Group, Georges Bank Petroleum Study, p. 35.

13. Any deepwater port in the United States would conform to and participate in the Council of Environmental Quality, "National Pollution Contingency Plan," Federal Register (February 10, 1975).

14. M.I.T. Offshore Oil Task Group, The Georges Bank Petroleum Study, pp. 74-75.

15. Norman C. Rasmussen, Draft Reactor Safety Study: An Assessment of Accident Risks in U.S. Commercial Nuclear Power Plants (Washington, D.C.: U.S. Atomic Energy Commission, August 1974).

16. D. S. Allan, A. A. Brown, and P. Athens, "Risks Associated with an LNG Shipping Operation," presented at the Fourth International Symposium on Transport of Hazardous Cargoes by Sea and Inland Waterways, New Orleans, La., April 1975.

17. Arthur D. Little, Analysis of Probability of Collisions, Rammings and Groundings of the LNG Barge Massachusetts, a report to Brooklyn Union Gas Company, Consolidated Edison Company of New York and Distrigas Corporation (Cambridge, Mass., October 1974).

18. D. S. Allan et al., op. cit.

19. Ibid.

20. M.I.T. Offshore Oil Task Group, The Georges Bank Petroleum Study, pp. 1-43 a.

21. V. F. Keith and J. D. Porricelli, "An Analysis of Oil Outflows Due to Tanker Accidents," Prevention and Control of Oil Spills, Proceedings of a joint conference of the American Petroleum Institute, Environmental Protection Agency, and U.S. Coast Guard (Washington, D.C., March 1973).

22. U.S. Congress, Offshore Ports and Terminals.

23. J. J. Henry Company, An Analysis of Oil Outflows Due to Tanker Accidents, 1971-1972, prepared for the U.S. Coast Guard (Springfield, Va.: National Technical Information Service, 1973).

24. U.S. Congress, Offshore Ports and Terminals, p. 114.

25. Ibid., p. 148.

26. Noel Mostert, Supertanker (New York: Alfred A. Knopf, 1974).

27. Keith and Porricelli, "An Analysis of Oil Outflows Due to Tanker Accidents," p. 8.

28. J. J. Henry Company, op. cit., p. 7.

29. Dames and Moore, Environmental Analysis of Louisiana Offshore Oil Port, prepared for LOOP (Washington, D.C.: U.S. Coast Guard, October 1975); SEADOCK, Inc., Application for License, 5 vols. (Washington, D.C.: U.S. Coast Guard, 1975).

30. U.S. Congress, 93rd, 2nd session, HR 10701, An Act printed with amendments of the Senate, October 9, 1974, p. 55.

31. Ibid., p. 66.

32. Ibid.

33. M.I.T. Offshore Oil Task Group, The Georges Bank Study, p. 55.

34. Ibid., p. 115.

35. Ibid., p. 109, 116.

36. The size of spill and spreading relationships are summarized in National Academy of Sciences, Petroleum in the Marine Environment, pp. 43-45.

37. SEADOCK, Inc., Application, 3:3-18.

38. Ibid., p. 6-2.

39. Dames and Moore, Environmental Analysis, Chapter 5, pp. 78-91.

40. Special Joint Subcommittee on Deepwater Port Legislation, U.S. Congress, Senate, Deepwater Port Act of 1973, S. 1751 and S. 2232, Serial 93-59, 93rd Cong., 1st session, 1973, p. 668.

41. Deepwater Port Act of 1974, pp. 65-66.

42. Initial regulations are contained in U.S. Department of Transportation, "Deep Water Ports," Federal Register 40, no. 217 (November 10, 1975).

43. Documents comprising LOOP, Inc., Application for License and studies relied on by SEADOCK, Inc., Application for License.

44. Nelson-Smith, op. cit., p. 48.

45. U.S. Department of Transportation, "Certain Tank Vessels: Proposed Rules," Federal Register 41, no. 74 (April 15, 1976). The Coast Guard is considering the addition of existing tank ships, but the decision appears to be based on the incentive and receptivity to a reduction in tank ship capacity during a period of oversupply.

46. Ibid., p. 40.

47. Ibid.

48. Statement by Russell Train before the U.S. Congress, Senate Committee on Commerce, 1973 IMCO Conference on Marine Pollution from Ships, 93rd Cong., 1st session, November 14, 1973, p. 11.

49. This assessment is presented in Exxon, Reducing Tanker Accidents (New York: Public Affairs Department, September 1973), pp. 14-17.

50. U.S. Congress, 1973 IMCO Conference on Marine Pollution from Ships, p. 5.

51. Office of Technology Assessment, Oil Transportation by Tankers (Springfield, Va.: National Technical Information Service, July 1975), pp. 4, 39-54.

52. U.S. Department of Transportation, "Certain Tank Vessels," p. 15861. Coast Guard sets rules pursuant to Ports and Waterways Safety Act of 1972.

53. Office of Technology Assessment, op. cit., p. 80.

54. U.S. Department of Commerce, Maritime Administration, "Tanker Construction Program."

55. Noel Mostert, op. cit., Chapter 8.

56. Office of Technology Assesssment, op. cit., p. 43.

57. Ibid., p. 166.

58. Ibid., p. 159.

59. J. J. Henry Company, op. cit., Appendix Table B-1.

60. Improvement in both operations are recognized by the Office of Technology Assessment, op. cit., pp. 54-72.

61. National Academy of Sciences, Petroleum in the Marine Environment, p. 106.

6

ONSHORE ENVIRONMENTAL
IMPACTS

Onshore impacts are difficult to assess because their quantification is a result of a series of decisions. A further problem is that the numbers themselves are rarely an adequate index to a reasonable assessment of the ecological consequences of refining and petrochemical plant siting. The Arthur D. Little study has covered the emission profile that would result at the level of petroleum processing, which that study has assumed.[1] What is not clear is the consequence of this emission profile in terms of its ecological significance or its impact on community values. The Little study did confirm that there is a fairly direct relationship between the level of refining activity and the emission quantities produced. More refineries will produce increased air pollution and may add more effluent to rivers and streams. Refinery activities will add jobs and increase tax ratables, but adequate treatment of these concerns is primarily site and project specific.

The specific air-quality parameters of concern are the addition of sulfur oxides, particulate matter, nitrogen oxides, hydrocarbons, aldehydes, and carbon monoxide. Each of these pollutants, with the exception of aldehydes, is a common ambient air-quality problem associated with industrial and transportation activity. The carbon monoxide emissions are generally localized and the contribution of the refinery is small enough and remote enough not to be considered in depth. The four remaining pollutants (sulfur oxides, particulates, nitrogen oxides, and hydrocarbons) could be measured in such a way as to estimate the contribution of petroleum processing in a local area compared to all emissions from all sources in that area. How these assessments are managed will be discussed, but the analysis starts with an emissions inventory. The refinery's contribution to such an inventory is shown in Table 6.1.

TABLE 6.1

Estimated Air Pollution Loads from a Typical 100,000 B/D
Integrated Refinery
(lbs/day)

Pollutant	Present Emissions	"New Source" Emissions
Particulates	12,000	800[a]
Sulfur oxides	25,000	4,300[a]
Nitrogen oxides	35,000	No change
Hydrocarbons	13,500	No change[a]
Aldehydes	1,000	
Ammonia	2,000	
Carbon monoxide	891,000 (uncontrolled)[b]	Nil[a]

[a]Based on 65,000 barrel/day fluid catalytic cracking unit regenerator meeting a standard of 0.022 grains per dry standard cubic foot for particulates; and 20 grains per standard cubic foot for sulfur dioxide of fuel gas burned assuming the refinery produces 15×10^6 dry standard cubic feet of process gas. For hydrocarbons floating roof tanks are assumed for all storage vessels reducing emissions to 4 pounds per 1,000 barrels stored. Actual emissions depend upon volume stored. Carbon monoxide emissions are reduced to nearly zero (stack emissions are below ambient air quality standards) through complete combustion.

[b]Based on a 65,000 b/d catalytic cracker.

Sources: Environmental Protection Agency, Compilation of Air Pollution Emission Factors (Research Triangle Park, N.C., 1972); Arthur D. Little, Potential Onshore Effects of Deepwater Oil Terminal-Related Industrial Development, 5 vols. (Springfield, Va.: National Technical Information Service, 1973), 5:154; Environmental Protection Agency, Atmospheric Emissions from the Petroleum Refining Industry (Research Triangle Park, N.C., August 1973), p. 31; "New source" emissions: Environmental Protection Agency, Background Information for Proposed New Source Performance Standards, 3 vols. (Research Triangle Park, N.C., June 1973).

TABLE 6.2

Estimated Water Pollution Loads from a Typical
100,000 B/D Integrated Refinery
(lbs/day)

Water Pollutant	Treatment Level	
	Presently Accepted	Advanced
BOD[a]	1,200	400
COD[a]	7,300	2,000
Oils	800	250
Total dissolved solids[b]	45,000	45,000
Suspended solids	3,500	600
Ammonia (as N_2)	400	40
Chromium	5	3
Phenol	50	5
Sulfides	10	2
Heat[c]		

[a]BOD = biological oxygen demand; COD = chemical oxygen demand.

[b]Under no wastewater discharge, approximately 10,000 tons per year dried salts would be produced, equivalent to 5 acre feet per year.

[c]"Cooling towers have played an important role in reduction of total thermal load primarily by reduction in quantities of water discharged and not necessarily by reduction in effluent temperature" (Jones).

Sources: Arthur D. Little, Potential Onshore Effects of Deepwater Oil Terminal-Related Industrial Development, 5 vols. (Springfield, Va.: National Technical Information Service, 1973), 5:147; Harold R. Jones, Pollution Control in the Petroleum Industry (Park Ridge, N.J.: Noyes Data Corporation, 1973), p. 139.

A second major onshore impact concerns the impact on water quality. There are several indexes of water quality for bodies of water and there are certain effluent emission limitations that can be imposed on refineries.[2] The primary concern of refineries is the waste load measured by biological oxygen demand (BOD), chemical oxygen demand (COD), total dissolved solids (TDS), and suspended solids (SS). These waste loads are common to all industrial processes. Another important discharge is oil. These discharges are presented under two treatment conditions in Table 6.2. As with air pollution, the ecological impact on a segment of river or some other water body cannot be determined without an inventory of waste loads. Although complex models have been used to show how wastes enter and diffuse in water bodies, even the results from these in-depth studies are specific to the area under consideration. Rather than attempt to continue to calculate effluent loads, it may be more profitable to put the air quality and water quality discussion in the context of how environmental degradation is or can be measured as a tool for impact analysis. Such a focus will allow consideration of a range of factors that are brought to bear in land-use decisions.

A third factor of diminishing importance in water-plentiful areas is the demand and use of water for refining. Since refineries have historically located near water access, the demand for water has not been a major obstacle in the Gulf or East Coast; the demand for water is declining on the basis of water use per barrel of oil refined.

A fourth environmental factor is the land-consumption requirements of petroleum storage. Petroleum companies often seek much larger parcels than they need for actual operations. Land is sought for future growth and as a buffer to nearby activities. The actual refinery processes (referred to as battery limits) use less than 10 percent of the land acquired for most refineries.[3]

A fifth impact to be discussed in this chapter is the job-creation aspects of refineries and petrochemical plants. The assessment will discuss some multiplier effects on community jobs and income, but the secondary urbanization effects on schools, roads, and taxes will not be covered. These latter developments are important, but again they are community specific and depend upon the level of activity.

COMMON METHODS IN IMPACT ANALYSIS:
AIR AND WATER QUALITY

Certain techniques are common to detailed evaluation of impacts. Few of these techniques were or could be used in the Little

study. These techniques are designed to take a calculated or measured level of emissions (or loads) and to relate them to a standard
that can be measured in the ambient air or measured in a body of
water. These techniques are well described in model-building de-
signs. The principles of such impact analysis are common to both
air and water quality.

The discharges from the pollution source are measured in
weight or in parts per million from the discharge pipe or from the
stack. These discharges then diffuse into the air or water body.
As neither the ambient air nor water environment are static, the actual impact of this diffusion varies through time and space. Through
biological studies the scientific community is asked to formulate a
consensual position on standards by which pollution levels are safe
in the long run and the short run. With these standards and with the
effluent discharge data, the objective of impact analysis is to show
how the effluent discharges diffuse and alter the measured ambient
levels in relation to the predetermined safe standards.

This extremely simplified explanation implies two requirements of a thorough impact analysis. One requirement is to have a
community-wide inventory of emission sources by which one begins
to scale or model the contribution of a specific source, such as a
refinery. Through the Environmental Protection Agency requirement to have an air quality control plan, such inventories are being
created, updated, and improved. For some years rivers and lakes
have been surveyed to determine the source and nature of effluent
discharges. Nevertheless, the existence of an inventory for water
or air does not testify for either its completeness or its accuracy.
The second requirement implied by impact analysis concerns diffusion modeling. Despite the elegance and continued theoretical ad-
vance in model building, it takes several years to successfully cali-
brate such environmental models so that output and in-stream mea-
surements begin to take on similar profiles.[4]

When such models are successfully calibrated they are specific
to an area. As a result of an inventory and diffusion calibration
problem, there are few areas where impact analysis can be readily
undertaken without extensive baseline studies. Decisions do not wait
for such studies, but the criteria for decisions become somewhat uncertain without such information. When emissions or loads are related to a standard concentration that even ambiguously pertains to
health and welfare then the impact analysis decision criteria become
more certain. Otherwise, it is only possible to scale in a rough percentage how much more or less of a certain quantity of a pollutant
there will be.

Useful impact analysis tied to administrative decisions is expensive and takes time. In the end such work becomes attuned to

managing an area--a river basin, an estuary, a coastal zone, or an air-quality region. Specific siting decisions are only adequately submitted to quantification when all the scientific and computation machinery are in place. Otherwise, quickly needed and persuasive advice requires a crash effort whereby a disparate group of experts from various disciplines are asked to develop a consensual position. The machinery for coastal zone management is only gradually becoming part of the administrative decision apparatus.[5] Both Texas and Louisiana are working on a coastal management plan as a prerequisite of state planning for a deepwater port. By comparison, the Environmental Impact Statement (EIS) and the Clean Air Act are already well along in the administrative machinery.[6]

It is asserted here that so far the primary impact of "environmental legislation" has been to provide a basis to submit site decisions to judicial review. As a result, the executive branch has to be more careful, even if decisions are only gradually being made in a more informed technical context. As projects have been set back by court decisions, the technical level of environmental analysis has improved; although the environmentalist as "watchdog" would appear to have been more effective in impacting decisions than the environmentalist as scientist. The onshore impact analysis of a deepwater port will consequently be faced with several criteria hurdles. These hurdles may be summarized as such prior to further consideration of impacts:

1. The administrative decision hurdle whereby legislation of the Deep Water Port Act of 1974 directs the administrator to comply with an evolving set of regulations and rules.

2. Scientific fact-finding hurdle whereby the best ecological information must be brought to bear on a terminal refinery and petrochemical plant location decision.

3. The decision process hurdle whereby the siting decision is submitted to a review-and-approval process before final project clearance is granted.

4. Political acceptability hurdle, which includes evaluation of the major actors and relative community attitudes.

Impact analysis concerns all four elements, as each in a separate way represents a set of criteria by which "impacts" are assessed. The criterion 4 is to some extent an evaluation of impacts as "perceived," which in the absence of previous experience by the "impacted" community depends upon received attitudes. The process criterion 3 pertains to how different groups gain access to influence in the siting decision. In each step of the process a somewhat different mix of interests is able to delay, alter, stop, or move ahead the process of obtaining the authority to proceed with construction. The first and second criteria are by logic one and the same, but because of the slow process of administrative and scientific interface these criteria are separated in fact if not in theory. The scientific community is consulted about whether a project represents a reasonable environmental risk with minimized impacts (criterion 1), but only through the administrative process is a set of evidentiary findings on impacts (criterion 2) brought forth as a basis for administrative and judicial decisions.

Port project plans are moving along in the Gulf Coast primarily because such projects are viewed as desirable by the majority of people in those states and regions. The scientific community in these states has been consulted, and a number of impact studies were produced by this community.[7] Studies are continuing in Texas and Louisiana. Fact-finding and the community-acceptance process can reasonably proceed ahead in order to determine the best location of a terminal.* Whatever congruence there may be on how impacts can be reduced, the administrative criteria upon which a license is issued must consider whether the "facts" fit future East Coast circumstances, in addition to whether the ports are "acceptable" on the Gulf Coast. In other words, the criteria for decision must be reasonably consistent insofar as federal agencies are concerned. Without this common basis, the environmental-impact evaluation can be successfully challenged as being based solely upon political acceptability. As a result, the whole process of government, in reaching a decision about licensing a port, considers acceptability of its various constituent parts. Neither the Gulf Coast nor the East Coast siting decisions can get too far ahead or behind the other. There may be a reasonable difference in interpretation of the facts and different groups are able to gain influence on a decision at different points in the process. By decentralizing the process somewhat through state-government veto, the deepwater port siting process allows greater regional variation in licensing. This decentralization does not increase the number of actors, but it does change the relative roles of the actors.

On the basis of scientific evidence, it would be difficult to understand how deepwater ports could be built on the Gulf Coast but could not be built on the East Coast. Federal agencies could not reach such a decision. Through availing the state the veto power, such action is possible. If two adjacent states disagreed about a

---

*This assumes that the ecological evidence supports the conclusion that a port is not a threat to the environment, but that some sites are clearly better than others.

port on the East Coast it is likely that the "facts" would be settled
in court. State veto does allow the process to move faster in areas
where ports are acceptable and slower where acceptability is still
in doubt. The relative speed of the process may itself be an effective device for increasing or decreasing the probability that a port
would be built. If the process is too cumbersome, few serious proposals will be submitted.

Under the circumstances, impact analysis represents one set
of facts upon which decisions are based. The crucial impacts may
be different in each case, although there will be some set of impacts
common to all decisions. It is not clear that state veto is necessarily based on a specific set of criteria; rather the decision may be described in relative terms of benefits and costs for which there is no
agreed procedure of calculation when environmental values are included. Often impact analysis is most effective when it attempts to
answer questions as they arise from those who are most affected by
the proposal. To some extent this requires anticipation of likely
impact questions. Often these questions have to do with reducing
uncertainty and minimization of risk, rather than the level of every-
day effluent loads.

LIKELIHOOD OF PETROCHEMICAL ACTIVITY

A major impact is to what extent refineries on the onshore
side of deepwater ports will be geared to gasoline or other final
products sold to existing establishments in the market area. Impacts are likely to be greater where the refinery is in an export
position relative to the regional market. In such a "surplus" position increased petrochemical activity is likely. In assessing the
petrochemical impacts, the Little study used the base data shown in
Table 6.3.

Although the Little study assumed that these loads are from a
"typical" petrochemical complex, its use and comparison with a
100,000 b/d refinery (Tables 6.1 and 6.2) is misleading. The scales
of the refinery and petrochemical plant do not fit each other. In order to produce the chemicals noted in Tables 6.3 and 6.4, considerably more refineries would have to be in place in an area, or the
raw materials for the chemical plant would be imported. The mix
of refinery outputs that would be consistent with the inputs needed by
the "typical" petrochemical plant would require 300,000 to 400,000
b/d refineries.

One possibility is that the petrochemical decision is assumed
to be a result of a deepwater port decision where crude is directly
available to the petrochemical plant. A second possibility on the

TABLE 6.3

Estimated Water Pollution Loads from a Typical Petrochemical Complex

	Ethylene	Ethylene Glycol	Vinyl Chloride Monomer	Polyvinyl Chloride	Ethanol	Polyethylene	Polyester Fiber	SBR Rubber	Total
Capacity	1,000MM lbs./yr.	300MM lbs./yr.	500MM lbs./yr.	300MM lbs./yr.	170MM lbs./yr.	400MM lbs./yr.	30MM lbs./yr.	50MM tons/yr.	--
Water usage (MGD)	6.5	2.5	2.5	2.0	1.0	2.0	1.5	2.0	20
Wastewater loads (lbs/day)									
BOD									
P	60	280	60	350	200	1,200	140	900	3,190
A	25	100	25	150	90	350	60	100	900
COD									
P	3,000	5,600	1,300	900	700	2,400	300	1,800	16,000
A	1,100	2,800	700	450	300	1,000	150	800	7,300
Oils									
P	1,500	--	--	--	100	--	--	--	1,600
A	200	--	--	--	20	--	--	--	220
TDS									
P	27,000	15,000	9,500	16,000	3,800	8,000	6,000	12,000	97,300
A	Same	Same	Same	Same	Same	Same	Same	Same	Same
SS									
P	200	neg.	--	500	--	1,200	60	450	2,410
A	60	--	--	200	--	300	20	50	630

P = presently available technology (equivalent to secondary treatment)

A = advanced technology (equivalent to tertiary treatment)

MGD = thousand gallons per day

BOD = biological oxygen demand
COD = chemical oxygen demand
TDS = total dissolved solids
SS = suspended solids
MM = million

Source: Arthur D. Little, Potential Onshore Effects on Deepwater Oil Terminal-Related Industrial Development, 5 vols. (Springfield, Va.: National Technical Information Service, 1973), 5:161.

Gulf Coast is a large refinery "surplus" in Texas and Louisiana that could provide refinery output as raw materials for petrochemical products. Neither condition now exists on the East Coast, but eastern Canada could move into the second refinery surplus position.[8] The Caribbean is already in a position of importing crude for export to the United States, in addition to export of products and crude from South American domestic sources.

TABLE 6.4

Summary: Estimated Air Pollution Loads Associated with a Typical Petrochemical Complex

Emission	Amount
	(pounds per day)
Particulates	17,000
Sulfur oxides	33,590
Nitrogen oxides	56,920
Hydrocarbons	24,170
	(millions of pounds per year)
Operations include:	
Ethylene	1,000
Ethylene glycol	300
Vinyl chloride monomer	500
Polyvinyl chloride	300
Ethanol	170
Polyethylene	400
Polyester	30
SBR rubber	10

Source: Arthur D. Little, Potential Onshore Effects of Deepwater Oil Terminal-Related Industrial Development, 5 vols. (Springfield, Va.: National Technical Information Service, 1973), 5:163.

Accordingly, the "typical" petrochemical plant in this instance is rather large. It is assumed that such a plant would not be built unless there were either: (1) an overwhelming regional market that could be served efficiently; (2) a secure incremental raw materials supply; or (3) a low-cost producing area where the long-term future of petrochemical production is not in doubt. Without a deepwater port the East Coast may meet the first condition, but this condition has existed for some time.

In 1967 the Middle Atlantic region contributed 15 percent and New England 3 percent of the value added to the petrochemical industry.[9] If a deepwater port were built, then the petrochemical plant of this size might find it cheaper to depend upon refinery output. On the other hand, if refineries were restricted to on-site expansions on the East Coast, then a very large chemical company might seek access to crude supply directly from the deepwater terminal. These uncertainties imply that a petrochemical plant sited on the East Coast would be built at less than maximum efficient size and thereby produce effluent loads about half of those in Tables 6.3 and 6.4. The investment in smaller and more flexible plants would be expected in the absence of direct access to crude via a deepwater port.

Site selection represents a difficult problem in light of concern about waterway pollution and coastal-zone ecology. Since a great amount of air and water pollution already exists along the East Coast, the best case for future plants is that a specific activity will not produce a measurable degradation in air and water quality. Clearly, such a case is not as easily made when plant size is geared solely to that level of output which minimizes unit cost of production. Market uncertainty alone might rule out the least-cost-production plant size. Perhaps the minimum environmental criterion for an East Coast grass roots refinery or petrochemical plant is that such a facility is not making air and water quality worse. This demonstration might involve a comparison of pollution loads eliminated by plant closedowns, compared to new loads from plant start-ups. Along polluted rivers it may be possible to return water from effluent discharge as clean as the water from the intake pipe. In areas of high air pollution this "zero degradation" might be achieved through buffer zones, which would not increase air-pollutant exposure among the general population because of diffusion characteristics.

Away from highly urbanized areas, a refinery will produce an incremental increase in effluent loads and air-pollution emissions. Crucial to nonurbanized areas are the relative conservation values of the area impacted--recreation, ecological significance, and other measures of environmental values. If possible, new plants can be combined with a reclamation activity, for example, siting facilities in areas where the remains of previous industrialization can be restored for historical interest or removed. The nonurbanized siting decision can reduce impacts by siting on marginal land; the urbanized site requires a good deal of buffering of adjacent activities and making the site perform additional services not necessarily associated with the cost of production. As a result, a persuasive or judgmental evaluation of impacts is more highly variable depending upon what is specifically proposed than on a predetermined likely profile of pollutant loads.

The evaluation of likely impacts would have to consider the following:

1. Whether the loading was an incremental increase in the area-wide emissions inventory; in highly urbanized areas with industrial activity the effect of one or two plants may be small relative to existing levels.

2. For air quality, new-source standards would have to be met and advanced wastewater treatment would be used.

3. The plant would have to buy considerable land for buffer zones and it would be beneficial to alter the site to conform to local desires (low tank profiles, screening).

4. The political jurisdiction would have to consider communities downwind from the plant, the air-quality control region in which the plant is located, emerging declaration of compatibility with coastal zone considerations, and regional air-quality control plans.

5. Potential fuel oil refinery's siting would consider location of customers; refineries that supply utilities would be evaluated for their potential to supply clean-burning fuel relative to existing supply. The product-surplus position of a refinery would be reviewed for its ability to induce petrochemical siting.

These studies represent the baseline from which change is measured. Without the inventory and without monitoring, it is difficult to bring meaning to impacts. It is possible to make assumptions about typical profile, but such analysis is little more than computation beyond the point of showing how the level of petroleum activity is derived. As noted in the Little study, their impacts are merely illustrative. As a result, planning organizations tend to focus their activity on baseline and inventory information, while concentrating on their model capability. Accordingly, as proposals are made the impacts can be cranked out to fit the circumstances.

SEADOCK and LOOP

Using SEADOCK's estimate of high case-induced refinery capacity of 1.62 million barrels, there would be 292,000 barrels a day feedstock for chemical plants. Their estimate is that this 18 percent feedstock availability would result in six new chemical plants by 1985. This estimate represents an upper limit on induced refining and chemical activity.

Such additional petrochemical processes would be spread
across 15 counties concentrated along coastal areas. The impact
on hydrocarbons and nitrogen oxides would be significant. Air quality would deteriorate given the inability of new-source refinery emissions, and truck contribution of hydrocarbons and nitrogen oxides
would decline relatively, but a growth in vehicle miles traveled will
mitigate gains from vehicle standards. It would not be unreasonable
to predict that photochemical smog will be as much or more of a
problem by 1985, given that oxidants and hydrocarbons are the major
ingredients of smog.

The Houston-Galveston area already exceeds, as do the New
York-New Jersey and Connecticut regions, the oxidant standards
measured by the Chemlunisence Method. The control of hydrocarbons and oxidants is a regional and interstate problem. In the Hous-
ton area, EPA has estimated that 73 percent of the hydrocarbons
originate from petroleum refining, chemical plants, petroleum storage, and handling.[10] The remainder come from vehicle sources.
New-source emissions do not appreciably reduce either hydrocarbons or oxidants with the exception of the changeover from fixed-
roof to floating-roof petroleum storage. EPA estimates that from
1975 to 1985 hydrocarbons from motor vehicles can be reduced 69
percent per vehicle and oxides of nitrigen can be reduced 50 percent.[11] Even with this per-vehicle improvement, more refining,
chemical plants, and more vehicles on the road are likely to more
than make up for any gains in automotive technology. In the New
York metropolitan region, where about 60 percent of the hydrocarbons and 40 percent of the nitrogen oxides are from vehicles, the
potential for cleaner air rests more with transportation. Along the
Texas coast the smog problem rests squarely with the petroleum
and chemical industry. The ability to develop air-pollution technology for these industries is the key to clean air or at least relatively clean air. The Texas area is then in contrast to other metropolitan regions because clean air cannot rely on the evolution of non-
polluting vehicles or reduced auto travel by commuters.

Both projects estimated the direct loss of land due to the requirements of petroleum storage, pipeline access, and other facilities. SEADOCK estimated that 860 acres would be lost onshore,
including 91 acres of marsh. The LOOP project estimated that biological production would be lost on 700 acres of swamp forest habitat.
A further consequence of salt-dome storage would be an increase in
salinity in the area of brine discharge. The estimate of increased
salinity was from 2 to 3.05 percent in three years. The LOOP environmental report stressed that the biological damage would remain
local, depending upon the nature of secondary development primarily,
rather than the direct disruption from construction and operation of
the port.

IMPACT ON JOBS

Refining and petrochemical activity will add jobs and will induce other activities, as well as inducing jobs in associated areas. The second "induced" impact may be more effectively measured by an income multiplier, since induced jobs can be quite elusive. Income multipliers are as difficult to trace, but at least aggregate changes can be detected and then attributed to various sectors of the economy.

The petroleum and chemical industries have been increasing in productivity and consequently the employment per unit of production has been declining. Little found that the petrochemical industry was increasing output per worker at 5 percent a year in the 1960s and forecast increases of 3.0 to 3.5 percent per year.[12] Refining industry is forecast to increase productivity at 3.5 to 4.0 percent per year. As a result, the employment per dollar of sales or per barrel of oil refined, will be less in the future. In 1970, the value of shipments in refining was $23 billion; value added by the industry was $4.6 billion and employees numbered 108,500, although some of these employees were actually engaged in petrochemical rather than refining activity. In 1970 the petrochemical industry contributed $19 billion in goods sold, value added of $10 billion, and employed 314,000.[13]

In looking at refining employment trends, the number of employees (per 1,000 barrels refined) is declining. A time series compiled by Kaiser and Gulf research yields the following trends in the average for Louisiana: 16.4 employees per thousand barrels refined in 1961, 12.1 in 1965, 8.2 in 1970, and 4.7 in 1975. This latter estimate and future estimates are based on new refineries adding employees at a rate of 2.5 to 3.5 per 1,000 barrels. The forecast is 4.2 per 1,000 in 1980, 3.7 in 1990.[14] Little assumed that for every 250,000 b/d refinery added, 550 employees would be hired in 1985.[15] This relationship yields 2.2 employees per 1,000, which assumes that refineries will be added in large increments.

Little assumed declining employment per million dollars of sales for petrochemical activity. The actual computation applied a 3.5 percent per annum productivity to the number of employees in their typical plant. This particular complex would employ 4,850 people in 1970. The Kaiser/Gulf study used a relationship between refining and petrochemical activity. The study found that this relationship was constant in Louisiana from 1965 to 1971, when jobs were increasing for both sectors. For every job in refining, there were 2.3 jobs added to the chemical industry.[16]

For construction jobs the Kaiser/Gulf study obtained estimates of employment gain due solely to the offshore port construction based

upon the LOOP proposal. The average number of construction jobs
for 1973-80 was 2,356, declining to 980 jobs for 1981-90. This estimate does not include construction jobs created by refinery or
petrochemical plant construction.[17] The addition of these latter employment components depends upon decisions to build refineries and
petrochemical plants. The Kaiser/Gulf assumptions were based
upon the addition of 617,000 b/d refining capacity to Louisiana
(1975-80) and the addition of 4.7 billion pounds of ethylene capacity.
These two assumptions yield the employment profile shown in Table
6.5. Based upon a shift-share analysis of employment, the study
assumed induced employment (Table 6.5), yielding a multiplier of
1.667, which was assumed to grow to 2.171 by 1990.[18]

TABLE 6.5

Estimated Employment (Direct and Indirect)
from a Deepwater Terminal

	Jobs
Deepwater terminal	
Construction: offshore	707
Operations: offshore	315
Refining (assuming addition of 617,000 b/d capacity)	
Construction	2,179
Operations	2,848
Petrochemical (assuming addition of 4.7 billion pounds of ethylene)	
Operations and construction	7,373
Subtotal	13,422
Induced employment (assuming a multiplier of 1.667)	21,970
Total	35,392

Source: H. J. Kaiser Company and Gulf South Research Institute, The Economic Impact of a Louisiana Offshore Oil Port
(Baton Rouge, La., 1973), pp. 44-53, Tables 24 and 25. Employment figures are considered for the entire state at estimated levels
of activity.

INCOME MULTIPLIER

Another way to look at economic impact is through an income multiplier. The statewide estimated effect of an offshore port in Louisiana was estimated to generate $374 million to the economy; again, this estimate assumed production levels from petroleum capacity increase of 617,000 b/d, and ethylene capacity increase of 4.7 billion pounds per annum. The increase in statewide income was 3 percent more with the port than without it in constant 1967 dollars.[19]

If the region under consideration were smaller, then the income added relative to the base would be larger, but the multiplier would be smaller due to leakages outside the region. It is also true that the income effects should be greater in a petroleum and chemical export state such as Louisiana compared to import states such as New York, Connecticut, or Massachusetts. For example, John M. Mattilla examined the export base in Detroit. From his model he found that the Detroit region had the following export income multipliers: 1.645 (machinery), 1.462 (fabricated metals), 1.504 (primary metals), 1.273 (motor vehicles), and 1.144 (chemicals). It is well known that the export multiplier will vary with size and industry mix or region.[20] Mattilla points out that, "Hansen and Tiebout obtained private export employment multipliers of 2.13 for Los Angeles/Long Beach, 2.06 for San Francisco/Oakland, and 2.76 for the State of California from input-output analysis."[21]

Whatever multiplier is assumed, the actual result depends upon where the port is constructed and the level of activity. Just as with air pollution and water pollution loads, the level of activity that is foreseen, or planned for, represents the critical factor.

The other element is technology. New technology and increased investment in reducing pollution show up in lower loads per unit produced. Both the new-source performance standard and the advanced wastewater treatment demonstrate this ability. Technology also reduces the number of jobs created per unit of production.

Having specified the technology, uncertainty still remains regarding the level of activity for which one is planning. As all impact levels depend upon activity levels, more effort and analysis should be devoted to planning for various levels of activity.

NOTES

1. Arthur D. Little, Potential Onshore Effects of Deepwater Oil Terminal-Related Industrial Development, 5 vols. (Springfield, Va.: National Technical Information Service, 1973).

2. Ibid., 5:146-51.

3. W. L. Nelson, "Cost of Refineries," Oil and Gas Journal (July 29, 1974).

4. For the relationship between models, administration, and water problems it is useful to focus on the Delaware River Basin Commission. There is more than 25 years' work on this important area beginning with Roscoe Martin, Guthrie Birkhead, Jesse Burkhead, and Frank Munger, River Basin Administration and the Delaware (Syracuse, N.Y.: Syracuse University Press, 1960). An analysis of water quality and decision making for the Delaware is provided by Bruce Ackerman and James Sawyer, "The Uncertain Search for Environmental Policy: Scientific Factfinding and Rational Decision Making Along the Delaware River," Environmental Law Review 1973 (New York: Clark Boardman, 1973), pp. 73-157. These latter authors are primarily concerned with the Delaware estuary comprehensive survey and successive efforts to define the water quality problem along the Delaware.

5. Code of Federal Regulations Coastal Zone Management Act, 16 U.S.C. 1451-64.

6. Code of Federal Regulations Clean Air Act, 42 U.S.C. 1957 et seq., and National Environmental Policy Act 42 U.S.C. 4321 et seq.

7. University of Delaware, Environmental Vulnerability of the Delaware Bay Area to Supertanker Accommodation, 4 vols. (Springfield, Va.: National Technical Information Service, 1973); State University of New York at Stony Brook, Possible Effects of Construction and Operation of a Supertanker Terminal on the Marine Environment in the N.Y. Bight (Springfield, Va.: National Technical Information Service, 1973); M.I.T., A Preliminary Assessment of the Environmental Vulnerability of Machias Bay, Maine (Springfield, Va.: National Technical Information Service, 1973); Texas A & M University, Environmental Aspects of a Supertanker Port on the Texas Gulf Coast (Springfield, Va.: National Technical Information Service, 1973).

8. U.S. Department of Interior, Petroleum Refineries in the United States (Washington, D.C.: Bureau of Mines, 1972).

9. Little, op. cit., 5:5-11, Table 5-5.

10. U.S. Senate, Subcommittee on Environmental Pollution, Committee on Public Works, Hearing, Implementation of Transportation Controls, 93rd Cong., 2nd session, Serial No. 93-H29 (Washington, D.C., 1974), pp. 243-303.

11. Environmental Protection Agency, Compilation of Air Pollution Emission Factors (Research Triangle Park, N.C., 1975), Appendix D, p. D.7-1.

12. Little, op. cit., 5: Appendix III, pp. 125-42.

13. Ibid., 5:3.

14. H. J. Kaiser Company and Gulf South Research Institute, The Economic Impact of a Louisiana Offshore Oil Port (Baton Rouge, La., 1973).

15. Little, op. cit., 5:50.

16. H. J. Kaiser Company and Gulf South Research Institute, op. cit., p. 43.

17. Ibid., p. 44.

18. Ibid., pp. 49-53.

19. Ibid., p. 54.

20. John M. Mattilla, "A Metropolitan Income Determination Model and the Estimation of Metropolitan Income Multipliers," Journal of Regional Science 13, no. 1 (1973).

21. Ibid., p. 10. See also W. L. Hansen and C. M. Tiebout, "An Intersectoral Flow Analysis of the California Economy," Review of Economics and Statistics 45 (1963).

Development implies change and often a kind of change that cannot be reversed and is not readily amenable to control by the individual or by the community in which he is a part. Sometimes development is welcomed or opposed because the consequences are known and measured. Often development is opposed because the consequences are not well known and there appears to be no easy way to control these less well-known consequences. A good part of the political process in capital and siting decisions focuses on reducing uncertainty, minimizing risks, and acting on the basis of perceptions.

Every important land-use decision in a federal system is carefully brokered, the information generated is brokered, and timing of events is brokered. A good part of this brokering is self-interest, but another purpose is to reduce risk. One risk-reducing technique is to provide many bureaucratic checks in the approval process by the requirement that a land-use decision proceed through application, information, and approval stages. By allowing several agencies to review the application, each agency will be given an opportunity to amend the proposal to fit its own mission and jurisdictional point of view.[1] For example, if there is some risk of oil spills then the Coast Guard is given lead-agency status; where offshore environmental impacts are in doubt, a role is provided to the National Oceanic and Atmospheric Administrator; and, where state expertise in land-use siting requires strengthening, then the coastal zone legislation is given additional funding. Other administrative techniques include submission of plans, development of new programs, initiation of new reporting procedures, and setting aside special funds for oil spills. A $100 million cleanup fund is a good example.

Much of this activity is designed to modify proposals, provide information, and provide exposure to the decision prior to and quite apart from the need to make a decision. The information generated and the steps that must be followed are often much less important for what they reveal than the reaction, public or private, that stems from such activity. The "decision" always awaits the nod from elected officials--governors, mayors, or the president, through the White House. Often these officials are less interested in what the information reveals than they are in what other key actors think about the decision.* Their concern for information extends to how information may reflect on the positions they take. Positions are carefully coordinated with the process. Information is supplied through the process, and statements by executive-branch officials are carefully delayed until every impact statement is filed, every view is sought, and all studies are completed.

Much land-use legislation is designed to sift information; more requirements are added in order to carefully reduce the actual risk and uncertainty. Progress is measured by how ably the bureaucrats and elected officials are able to narrow the factors upon which the decision is based. If there are too many considerations to deal with, then delay and further process requirements will expand and lengthen the search for an easier basis to decide.[2]

If a decision is not based on the information, then what is it based on? For the most part, it is based on the process of elimination of the doubtful benefits, reduction of the uncertainties, which, if they came to pass, would lead to regret. Land-use decisions are particularly those where regret is not personal, but obvious to many who have some knowledge of the alternatives.

One of the more underestimated factors in capital decisions is the extent to which decisions can be postponed. Projects that require construction time of three years could take 15 years to plan, negotiate, review, and modify. In the meantime, costs escalate and the benefits of the project go unrealized. It is often difficult to understand whether anyone is serious about projects that are continuously approved, but somehow never happen. For the elected official, a capital project that may not be delivered within one or two terms of office is an elusive objective. Even where the decisions are made quickly regardless of the information-sifting process (and every effort is made to accomplish the objective), there may

----

*Indeed, chief executives make it a point to consult key political figures, sometimes publicly, in order to show that others implicitly concur or that all views are considered. At this juncture, the executive has completed his search for facts.

be no evidence that the elected official can point to that confirms his role. He or she may be quite amenable to cleaning up the air or improving public transportation, but the proof may lie many years away. Semblance of progress rather than the progress itself becomes important to the official in pursuing long-term goals.

DISTRIBUTION OF BENEFITS AND COSTS

Once uncertainty has been carefully delimited, land-use decisions are reviewed for who bears the cost and who receives the benefits. The scientist and engineer become less important as uncertainty is eliminated. The next requirement is to negotiate positions, alternatives, and influence in order to reach accommodation. When bargaining begins, only those groups which have a stake and weight ("clout") are seriously consulted. Game theory becomes an applicable model as local, state, and private interests bargain. Often there is no accommodation, as one party has the ability to impede or veto if unsatisfied.

Activity tends to shift to state and local groups. The legislature is less involved than the executive branch. Often new legislation and rules are written in order to readjust the pattern of bargaining in the accommodation process. In the earlier phase it was important to reduce the land-use decision to its essentials in order to specify what will or can happen. Once these bounds are set, positions become ambiguous because each participant to the bargaining process attempts to assess the other players' requirements without revealing his own. Impact analysis is no longer pertinent to decisions. From the point of view of game theory, this activity by government is an exploration of benefits and costs.* The ambiguity itself has some value as a screen. Budgets and positions do not identify the problem, but are instruments by which the process is played and recorded.

While these considerations are weighed inside government, there are external forces that alter the process. These include national events where federal constituents and policies are brought to bear, the courts where one of the ignored players seeks access to "clout," elections where decisions are required by deadlines or

---

*Benefit-cost analysis presumably provides a portion of the answer. Invariably the benefits and costs involve different values and different goals and objectives. The accommodation process is a way of shifting the benefits and costs so that a particular capital project has something for everyone.

required to be postponed, and finally, the element of newly elected officials.*

In a federal system it is often possible to go to another level of government to get action that is stalled somewhere else. Federal mass-transit agencies will deal with cities if states are not responsive. Environmentalists will go to the federal level, if local and state governments balk. By and large, it is in the executive branch and the courts where land-use decisions are centered. Legislative bodies provide the money and write the rules of the game. The executive branch interprets the rules and the courts are a check against executive actions.

Within the executive branch are agencies that promote their land-use perspective--environmental protection, planned development, commerce, highways, and so forth. Much of the strategy of these agencies is geared to getting commitments from elected officials, preferably commitments that cannot be undone by future elected officials. Acquiring land, letting contracts, designating areas, and initiating programs are means to these commitments, steps along the road to the objectives of the agency and the people who work within it.

Most of these latter actions relate to how benefits and costs are distributed when land-use decisions are made. There are many arenas in which leverage is sought. Unlike the uncertainty-reducing behavior described earlier, it is the latter activity that creates problems. Problems include bureaucracies with uncertain or changing missions whose former objectives are no longer serving the public adequately as well as unequal access to influence by certain single-purposed groups. Other difficulties entail unrealistic expectations based upon past commitments that are no longer possible to deliver to the constituents. Another difficulty is that the key players change more rapidly than the decision under review, and consequently each commitment is reviewed from scratch as a matter of course.

---

*Newly elected officials will often review capital commitments as a matter of general policy. Moreover, there may be specific commitments regarding projects that he or she has made during the election campaign. Since there are never enough capital funds to go around, dropping a project is not usually a problem. Adding one, however, creates problems of priorities. There are projects that will always be on plans without ever getting built because of commitments and priorities.

GENERALIZED PROBLEMS IN
CAPITAL CONSTRUCTION

Several outcomes can develop from a large development project such as a deepwater port. First, the factors that account for uncertainty and risk may not be adequately brought under control in the eyes of state and local government. As the decision to build a port on the Gulf Coast results in completion, this uncertainty may continue on the East Coast. Attitudes toward further industrialization, oil-spill risks, and land consumption for urbanization may be such as to defeat an East Coast project. This failure may be ascribed to the inability to plan. On the other hand, if many sites are investigated with the cooperation of local and state government, but each site is found wanting, then the decision not to build may be ascribed to a failure in accommodation. The failure to accommodate and the failure to plan relate to two slightly different problems. A failure to plan is the failure to reduce the uncertainty and risk factors to tolerable levels. It is also true that a decision to build (or not to build) judged in retrospect to be a mistake is also, and more commonly described as, a failure to plan. Before a decision is made, however, the failure to plan is the failure to reduce risks and uncertainty.

If those who make decisions are not scared off, then several other factors may affect a project. As capital projects take time, one failure common to public works is the failure to sustain commitment. This failure is not restricted to construction. It applies to conservation: acquiring parkland, maintaining lands and waterways in their natural state, or cleaning up the air or water. Whenever the objective is not manageable in a few years, there is the fate of reduced commitment or the objective itself may be altered to fit the need to perceive progress and sustain commitment.

For construction projects, several other consequences are possible. The cost of construction may outrun the benefits as delays and more expensive requirements are added to the project. For a public project the financing may just not be adequate, but it becomes politically difficult to admit this. For private projects, the environmental quid pro quo may be such that industry finds it cheaper to go somewhere else and build. Louisiana Senator Johnston continually asked at hearings if state government should not be allowed to tax deepwater ports in order to be repaid for some of the costs imposed on the people of the state. These demands on a private project are somewhat parallel to problems of escalating costs for public-sector projects.*

---

*The assumption here is that private projects, once begun, can be finished in a couple of years.

Assuming that a deepwater port can quickly get underway, that the cost of environmental safeguards and local government compensation are not too high, and that commitment can be sustained, then one essential obstacle remains. This obstacle is the misjudgment or the inability to accommodate the vital interest groups that must agree to the project.

Sometimes the rules are at fault. For example, existing land-use legislation may be too weak to provide strict guidelines. From the viewpoint of maintaining influence in a decision, there may be a point at which one or more groups feel they lose control over future events. (An example is the legal standing a group may have, where the law is explicit regarding how the court will rule in such cases.) Even if the proper balance can be maintained throughout the land-use siting process, legislation or the courts may be applying a set of rules by which one of the groups cannot abide. In these cases such groups are apt to refuse to be accommodated. They will rely instead on a political veto power away from the bargaining table.[3] Often, too, industry or the executive branch agency is unaware of whose interests are really at stake and the relative weight given to these interests. A company may quietly acquire land in a community and have leverage from the point of view of property law, only to be defeated in a public meeting where zoning is decided;* or, for example, the governor's favorable statement about a deepwater port may help enormously, but it may have no influence on the ability to obtain a specific site.

Overall, many groups will be satisfied through compensation of any losses that they may incur. Nevertheless, the more important interests (by definition) cannot be accommodated in this fashion. The reward for these groups may be in terms of satisfying certain principles that they hold, or allowing them to influence the course of events through consultation and mutual adjustment. Only those with their own substantial political influence assume they can deal with a few key players and isolate these single-purpose groups.[†] Industry and most agencies of government cannot afford this

---

*The Onassis proposal failed in New Hampshire in such a manner, but John McDonald cites the opposite example in Maine.

†An inverse relationship is assumed between how strongly any one goal is held and the multiplicity of goals groups or organizations hold. Multipurpose organizations would tend to be less "principled," that is, more willing to adjust and hence more easily accommodated than a single-purpose group. Consequently, single-purpose groups are given more attention by the bureaucracy, since the bureaucracy cannot usually presume to weight the "clout" these organizations have.

presumption and must be willing to adjust to all interested parties of a decision. The assumption that the path of resistance can be cleared up by a few key political people is only operational with a somewhat apathetic community.

Often it is those groups which at least profess to base their views in the public interest that have the most influence in particular aspects of a decision.* As long as the public-interest groups appear to be willing to be accommodated, some basis for accommodation is usually sought in the political process. When industry attempts to ignore this process and only deal with top governmental officials, then the seeds for their failure are sown.[4]

At times, however, there may be no on-going process to which a decision can be given. In such cases, the community and its political representatives are not equipped to set a decision-making process in motion. Sometimes this difficulty is one of timing and resources, and by slowing down events the accommodation decision-making process may be allowed to work. At other times, the decision appears to be both too big as well as too soon for local government. When this situation is apparent, the decision is usually referred to the governor or some higher level of government.

It is not always altogether clear when a higher level of government is acting in the lower level's behalf, or if such actions at the state level are merely designed to test local reaction or attempt to force a decision over local opposition. There is also the factor that the higher the level to which a decision is referred, the more important it is for that level to appear to have the power to make a decision. A decision on a deepwater port that very quickly reaches the governor's office is likely to reflect the need to slow down the decision process rather than to make a decision. Local government may be telling the governor that they don't like the pressure, and that by giving the problem to the governor, it is a way of relieving that pressure--"passing the buck." Once a decision reaches the governor's office after a long period of public exposure, the decision does not entirely ever leave the governor. He may invent or have forced upon him delaying steps (task forces, consultation with other parties) that provide time and build a case, or remove blame, for

---

*Public interest is defined somewhat more broadly than those groups having titles such as "public interest" or which have through the years developed a reputation for public interest. Among those included under the definition of public interest are: (1) self-styled public-interest groups which warn us of where the future is headed; (2) groups which chose a geographical area and a claim to know what is best for that area. In both instances, these groups speak for a public.

the eventual decision. But once this process takes its course, it is
difficult to retrieve the decision and place it back with local government.

At this point, local government is in a position of modifying
rather than stipulating. Accordingly, major decisions that arrive
too quickly at the state level are usually signs that local government
does not know exactly what to do, rather than any desire that the
governor of the state do anything. If the process has run its course,
then local government is concerned about what the governor will do,
and may attempt to retrieve the decision as a local one. It is often
the case that the governor is brought into a capital decision because
the locality needs financing rather than any desire that the state
make the decision.

PLANNING VERSUS PROCESS AND
PLANNING AS PROCESS

Because planning for projects such as a deepwater port has
been described as a problem of reducing risk and uncertainty, then
process is one means to achieve this end. Process is also a means
by which accommodation is made: budget process, zoning process,
hearing process, and other approval processes. The accommodation process and the planning process overlap at many points.

For some, process is planning, or all that planning should be.
Planners are expected by other local agencies and many other ob-
servers to conduct a "fishbowl" exercise in debate, plan making,
goal formulation, evaluation and assessment, monitoring, and
citizen participation as part of their functions. Since the accommodation aspects are normally taken over by others as their "policy
space," the planner is not considered to have influence in a decision. From inside government the planning organization often
appears to be inserting itself into the accommodation process,
where planning does not belong. This view is based upon the judgment that the planner has no constituency and therefore, cannot
"represent" anyone. From outside government a decision may
still be fraught with risks, or more likely, certain vital aspects
are perceived to be ignored, which outside groups feel the planners
should address. Outside groups perceive that planners are too
bound up in the accommodation process to provide the information
that is lacking.

For many, planning is more than process. It may be considered as the putting forth of the best technical advice and the bringing
out of factors regarding consequences or other considerations that
bear on uncertainty. It is when these elements are sought that the
planning function is distinct from the accommodation process.

Often the planning organizations must grope their way toward the technical part of planning. The information may exist somewhere else and the planner may be ill-equipped to obtain and interpret certain information. Again, the planning process can be called upon to institute discovery procedures regarding the cause and effect of land-use decisions. The failure to bring out the principal consequences of a land-use decision is a major fault in planning. Uncertainty and risk may become the chief obstacle to further consideration of development.

The alternative to development is likewise impacted by this inability. Mistakenly or otherwise, many of the environmental goals are not pursued to an operational level because of the failure to deal effectively with the economic consequences or other perceived difficulties of these environmental proposals. Attempting to prove that certain features of nondevelopment are beneficial may be just as difficult as proving that development can be controlled. Any movement from the existing situation is resisted by a major segment of a community.

As a result of the failure to plan in the sense of revealing consequences of decisions, there is some resistance to take on more process, particularly if the process itself does not lead to better information. The failure of government to effectively deal with land-use decisions is often the failure to design the process around the information needed. More often the planning process develops a kind of specious preview and leads into the accommodation process. Consequently, decisions are based on a poorly informed group of officials who are apt to feel at a disadvantage if they attempt to take any more than an incremental step away from the status quo.[5]

REVIEW OF DEEPWATER PORT SITING PROBLEMS

From the point of view of state government approval, deepwater ports may encounter one or more of the problems discussed. Some examples are given in the following list:

Planning Problems	Illustrative Examples
The inability to protect against a decision that the state may knowingly regret.	Failure to protect vital seashore recreation from a major oil spill.
The inability to reduce risk and uncertainty to tolerable levels.	No clear delineation between the decision to build a terminal, and the ability to withhold the approval of additional refineries and petrochemical plants.

The inability to provide information that would otherwise
impact on how risk is viewed.

Failure to examine, under the
auspices of state government, the
oil-spill potential of a deepwater
port compared to the potential
without such a port (relative risk).

The inability to design a process that would yield information on the consequences of a
deepwater port decision.

The deepwater port decision contains no procedural requirements
to show the linkage between port
throughput and refinery crude oil
needs.

Accommodation Problems

Illustrative Examples

The process is considered to
be faulty by certain key groups,
which consequently refuse to
be accommodated.

The governor takes the position
that his veto power over deepwater
ports will not be based on the need
to limit growth in the state.

One or more of the key groups
considers that the decision is
beyond their influence at some
point.

The governor is prohibited from a
conditional veto of a port proposal,
which restricts the site decision to
that proposed in the original application for a license.

The conditions for approval
put the proposal beyond a
viable range.

An "adjacent coastal state" conditions its approval on the stipulation
that the port be sited so that a
third adjacent state is needed as
participant to the decision.

The decision process isolates
key groups from participation.

The Council of Governments criti-
cizes the governor on the coastal-
zone plan for the state and recom-
mends against port approval.

The decision process fails to
accommodate key groups
through misjudgment about
their "clout."

The town council rescinds their
approval for a tank farm and adopts
a new land-use plan on the basis
of the presentation of air-quality
data by environmental groups.

The decision process is not
"geared up" to deal with a
problem of this scope.

The affected communities along the
coastal zone refuse to participate
in the statewide coastal-zone management plan. Few of the communities have a full-time staff.

The decision process moves the decision along too quickly for adequate review.

The governor announces the formation of a "state development zone" committee to handle the deepwater port license. The governor quickly reverses himself after heated local reaction, and announces that no ports would be built in the state.

These examples are hypothetical. The point is that the planning and accommodation problems are at least somewhat different. The planning aspects are prior to accommodation. Planning does not imply a purely technical element, planning also relies on procedure. This procedure is, or should be, based on its information value, rather than its accommodation value. In a "crisis" situation it is clearly difficult to separate accommodation and planning. These aspects are distinct and are designed to answer a separate set of questions. Without the information, the land-use decision rarely goes beyond the planning stage. Obfuscation and ambiguity are really more germane to accommodation. Those who seek accommodation already have their view in hand about risk and uncertainty.

The tendency to persuade while providing information only interferes with the planning process; to do anything but persuade during the accommodation process may be ineffective. The problem is to determine in what process one is engaging, or alternatively to understand what kinds of questions are being asked.

The deepwater port decision proceeds through several phases in a decision-making process. Much of this decision making can be described as politics. Much of it may also be considered planning. It is all governmental process. Planning would include aspects of providing information for decisions or revealing consequences of decisions. The information or knowledge generated also becomes a part of persuasion and accommodation.

The role information plays in a decision depends upon how the decision is viewed. From the point of view of closely examining what goes on prior to an announced decision, it may be concluded that information plays a minor role. From the perspective of how the basis for a decision shifts from decision point to decision point, information plays a crucial role. The reason is that the decision is not a singular affair but a series of decisions, each of which is based on a number of perceived facts. Viewed in the context of what we know today compared to what we knew one year ago, for example, it must be concluded that a certain amount of information was digested in order to bring us up to our present state of wisdom. The use of the collective "we" is indicative of what the information is designed

to achieve. There is always an individual who, last year, was at
our present state of wisdom today. In terms of making a decision,
this process of uncertainty reduction may take another year before
a decision is made. If a decision were made today, it may be quite
different from a decision postponed for one year. This timing depends a great deal upon the processes described in this chapter: the
planning process and the accommodation process.

From this discussion it is clear that the deepwater decision may
be quite different on the East Coast and the Gulf Coast. Governmental
processes and the time they take are crucial to these differences.

An attempt to describe and evaluate the factors germane to a
port decision is not the same as consideration of the basis on which
decisions are made. Very quickly, factors may become somewhat
incidental and the knowledge about deepwater ports may quickly go
beyond what is discussed here. On the other hand, there are always
aspects of a decision that require continual reexamination, and
whose importance should not be minimized.

It is concluded that these important aspects include petroleum
demand, oil-spill risks, and the separation of the refining and port-
siting decision. Ports would be better sited if they were designed to
serve existing demand. The savings generated from a well-designed
port are more than enough to pay for the additional costs of environmental protection. How ports are designed and built, and particularly how they are operated, represents the major factor in oil-spill
risks. Finally, the benefits of the port are commercial and the
environmental safeguards should be built into the monetary rewards
from such ports.

NOTES

1. It may be said that the agency can exercise its responsibility for its turf or "policy space." See Anthony Downs, Inside Bureaucracy (Boston: Little, Brown, 1967).

2. Another factor in addition to uncertainty is the ambiguous
nature of the legislative mandate. The administrator's position in
controlling the access of competing interest groups is made more
difficult if the terms of his mandate are highly ambiguous. Land-
use and capital decisions are in the more ambiguous areas of administrative behavior because they are specific actions usually
based on rather general legislative intent. David B. Truman,
The Governmental Process (New York: Alfred A. Knopf, 1951),
p. 443.

3. There is, of course, no game theory equivalent to a player
who refuses to play the game as described. This is an essential

problem of game theory since the players define the rules, or their limits, as events require. Only an astute political observer can describe the game adequately. For a game-theory treatment of deepwater port siting decisions in Maine see John McDonald, The Game of Business (Garden City, N.Y.: Doubleday, 1975), Chapter 14.

4. What is really meant is that industry deserves to fail. This may also be true for communities and regions that only rely on a few top officials (proximate decision makers) and subsequently regret the decisions. Peter Amory Bradford describes high political dealing in the Machias and other Maine projects in Fragile Structures: A Story of Oil Refineries. National Security and the Coast of Maine (New York: Harper's Magazine Press, 1975). The book is good political journalism because it describes who did what to whom regarding Maine refineries. Bradford shows in the Maine case that the environmental considerations were never valued at the higher-decision levels and only gradually became part of the state position.

5. A summary of these processes is described by C. E. Lindblom in the chapters "Making the Most of Analysis" and particularly "Strategies and Dodges" in The Policy Making Process (Englewood Cliffs, N.J.: Prentice-Hall, 1968), pp. 24-27. Lindblom's other works are also useful: C. E. Lindblom and D. Braybrooke, A Strategy of Decision (New York: The Free Press, 1963); Robert Dahl and C. E. Lindblom, Politics, Economics and Welfare (New York: Harper, 1953). Other works pertinent to the chapter include Aaron Wildavsky, The Politics of The Budgetary Process (Boston: Little, Brown, 1964), and J. G. March and H. A. Simon, Organizations (New York: John Wiley and Sons, 1958).

8

TENTATIVE FINDINGS

Although Congress has written the Deepwater Port Act, it is up to states, localities, and administrative agencies to decide whether and how ports will be built. The previous chapters have dealt with separate aspects of the deepwater port decision. The political process, however, concerns itself with only a few key issues at any one time.

Peter Bradford described the political maneuverings of the Maine deepwater port proposals from 1968 to 1974.[1] The chief obstacle to a Maine port and refinery was the Oil Import Program. The refinery represented a potential threat to the delicate balance of rewards that the petroleum companies had won over the years. The only serious governmental study of the Oil Import Program yielded the recommendation to abolish the quota system and institute a tariff. The recommendation was ignored by the Nixon administration, and the program became obsolete with the energy crisis.

The curious aspect of these events was the inappropriate basis for decision. Maine did not get a refinery because the environmentalists opposed it, but because it upset the major oil companies that would not share in the refinery benefits. After the quadruple of oil prices, a White House decision and program became transformed into a state land-use issue. Decisions that were centered in the White House, because of the access to power by multinational oil, lost national significance with the demise of the Oil Import Program.[2]

Even with this reprieve from White House machinations, Maine state government had little information about her oil company suitors' intentions. With a few exceptions noted by Bradford, state government gained by the opportunity to compare proposals of Occidental Petroleum and Richfield Oil, rather than through any systematic search for information by state government.

171

In Bradford's account no one in state government had the information and none seemed to be needed. Environmental values existed and these ideas spread, but information on better ways to site a deepwater port and refinery was generated in few quarters.[3] In the early going the idea was to get a refinery approved by Washington and then worry about planning later.

The economics of the Maine port decision changed with the energy crisis. And with that change some players were no longer dominant. The problem is that prediction of prices is not the only conventional wisdom that may be upset and lead to a different game. There will always be incomplete information. Predictions are rarely right. While the remedy for incomplete information is a process that works, the converse is rarely true.

FURTHER NOTES ON PROCESS

The process requirements would require as much, perhaps more, attention to the administrative agencies. No criteria and safeguards of legislative mandates can be taken for granted. The administration of a statute is, properly speaking, an extension of the legislative process. In looking at the role of interest groups in the administration of any given statute we may well inquire what it is that the administrator is extending.[4] States, localities, and environmental groups are wise to monitor the Deepwater Port Act mandate. The Coast Guard and other federal administrative agencies have discretion in many areas. More likely, however, is that the state itself may be short on administrative experience on deepwater ports. Most states will be ill-equipped to bolster their own processes while reviewing federal actions. It falls to interest groups of various kinds to mount the countervailing pressures on federal agencies. The petroleum industry, well versed in federal administrative processes, has the inside track.

Environmental trade-offs, as noted in Chapter 5, are linked to the reduction of risk. The better siting and planning proposals are likely to be generated through a wide search of alternatives. As the environmentalist was not a player in the Maine siting in 1968, the problem of keeping all players in the game is a monumental "process" task. The strategies or "dodges" that might be used to accomplish this wide search run counter to the need to make a decision. A wide search of alternatives usually implies delay, and delay is commonly thought of as a problem of bureaucracy. Nevertheless, risk and uncertainty reduction require considerable review.

From the point of view of preserving environmental values, the deepwater port game does not favor environmental protection.

It is not for the lack of environmentalists in the United States but for the very real problem that the site of a port is only one factor in reducing spills and air pollution. The petroleum companies can always go elsewhere, but environmental protection from a scientific perspective is not solely a U.S. coastal problem. A controlled decision on deepwater ports in the Gulf Coast is probably a better solution than a less-controlled design and operation outside the United States. Much of the environmental concern is not global, even if the environmental dilemma is global. The problem of process is the problem of extending environmental protection beyond the U.S. borders. Tankship operation, construction of ships, pollution conventions, and petroleum-company practices are somewhat outside the jurisdiction of states and regions. Multinational oil companies are by no means amenable to making it easier for states and regions to extend that control to reduce oil-pollution risks. Such compliance to state wishes interferes with international business, whose lowest common denominator is the relative cost to international commerce.

The deepwater port process protects the environment incompletely, partly because the environmentalist is oriented to his "turf." The major reason is that the world of tankship operation is beyond U.S. jurisdiction. Genuine environmental protection from oil spills may be in the national and international arena rather than the specifics of a port location. The political process is likely to overlook the international problem and focus on siting problems.

BENEFITS OF DEEPWATER PORTS

From the viewpoint of engineering, deepwater ports are not built to relieve existing facilities of excess demand. It is not likely that port turnaround will be greatly improved or that other capacity limitations will be affected.

The benefits of deepwater ports depend upon technological innovation. Very large crude carriers combined with offshore terminals create savings in the transport of oil. These savings depend upon the tankship market, the incremental cost advantage over existing handling, and the volume of oil delivered. In any case, the savings are significant, but they are small relative to the going price of a barrel of oil. A likely range of transport savings is 2 percent to 6 percent of the price of oil.

These savings are likely to be appropriated by the oil companies, OPEC nations, or the U.S. government. Consumers are not likely to see any reduction in prices, if for no other reason than the relative savings are small.

A state or region would have to look at the 15 cent to 40 cent
per barrel savings as the basis for claims to be set aside for environmental protection. A 2 cent per barrel surcharge has been
set up in the Deepwater Port Act of 1974. An important legal question is whether states can impose additional taxes beyond the federal
law. The courts have ruled against such taxes on the basis of regu-
lation of commerce, but have ruled that states can enact stricter
environmental standards than federal law.[5] It is clear that the only
possible basis for charges beyond the federal law is the environmental consideration.

Regions and states will not directly participate in deepwater
port savings except through the environmental funds. Even this participation is a contingency. Regional and state consumers are not
likely to see reduced prices for petroleum products.

With very little growth in petroleum demand, much of the need
for deepwater ports will be taken care of by the SEADOCK and LOOP
proposals. These two projects have the effect of concentrating development where it now exists. States and regions in the South,
Texas and Louisiana in particular, are mindful of the employment
and income benefits of a strong petroleum and chemical industry.
These two states and mid-West refinery areas along the Capline
pipeline and Mississippi River are locations likely to see continued
petroleum development. As much of the petroleum and chemical industries are located in these areas, the employment and income
benefits are likely to continue. These areas can attract secondary
and tertiary activities partially based upon foreign crude. Texas
and Louisiana are the main beneficiaries of further development
and can export to other regions.

Continued pressure for an East Coast site may arise from the
competitive forces of the smaller petroleum companies and the
terminal operators. With most of their oil-handling needs satisfied,
the major petroleum firms are not likely to be aggressive about an
East Coast site.

Two circumstances will contribute to major oil company interest: a desire to serve New York and Philadelphia refineries and
increasing petroleum consumption. The latter factor of increasing
consumption is not expected and only a change in outlook will make
states and communities more receptive to an East Coast port.

The smaller petroleum company and operator will continue to
seek access to Maine, owing to the deep water, relative undevelop-
ment, and extensive coast line. Interest in Maine will be moder-
ated by modest growth in consumption.

An alternative to serving the East Coast with an East Coast
site is to transship from Canada or the Bahamas. This alternative
may satisfy the major oil companies, as long as SEADOCK and
LOOP projects are built.

Overall, modest petroleum growth and Gulf deepwater ports will concentrate development and environmental impacts in the Gulf Coast. A terminal built on the East Coast, and particularly in Maine, is not expected to redirect the petroleum industry to the East. Consequently, few of the job and dollar benefits will accrue to East Coast states. For the East Coast, the major environmental impact will be the threat of oil spills, and not the secondary and tertiary developmental effects. No new petroleum centers will arise.

Only eastern Canada has developed the momentum of becoming a major refinery center. One 100,000 b/d refinery was built and another 150,000 b/d proposed for Port Tupper, Nova Scotia. Eastern Canada could develop a refinery export position even though the region is totally dependent on crude oil from other areas. If Canada were to complete a trans-Canadian pipeline, eastern Canada's use of foreign oil would have no strategic significance. Western Canada could export to the U.S. mid-West, and eastern Canada could refine for the U.S. East Coast without the spectre of foreign-oil dependence. Such a rise of eastern Canada as a refining center would only diminish the deepwater port attractiveness of Maine.

All of the factors mentioned tend to diminish the East Coast as an area of refining and chemical activity despite the potential of a deepwater port. Development will likely favor those areas that have had the head start--the Gulf Coast primarily and possibly Eastern Canada as a secondary center.

COSTS OF DEEPWATER PORTS:
EAST COAST AND GULF COAST

With LOOP and SEADOCK in place, an East Coast terminal is not likely to bring the secondary impacts. The threat of oil spills will remain, however, and products may be imported. Oil terminals may be built for transshipment, bringing no development but maintaining the oil-spill threat. One way or another the East Coast will import oil by water and the petroleum companies will use very large crude carriers to the extent that this saves on transport cost. If this use of the VLCC does not include an East Coast port, then some transshipment arrangements are likely.

Oil-spill potential will increase in the Gulf Coast. Both SEADOCK and LOOP will bring increased development along the coastal region. The Gulf Coast needs to be particular about how development affects coastal-zone water and air quality. Increasing use of foreign supplies will not diminish the Gulf Coast as a petroleum center, but it may very well prove harmful to the coastal environment. Environmental pressure will have to be put on state and local

government by those who depend upon the coast for their livelihood.
Petroleum refinery and transportation will interfere to some degree
with fishing and boating. Air quality should not be allowed to deteriorate. It is not likely that state standards will be stricter than
federal ones, nor is it likely that the industry will do better than it
does elsewhere. Environmental guardians will necessarily be self-
appointed.

Air pollution will continue to be a problem in coastal areas.
As development continues, photochemical smog will be a long-term
problem. The new-source performance standards do not envision
an improvement in either the hydrocarbon or nitrogen oxide standards.
(See Table 6.1.) Both the petroleum and chemical industries must
make the air-pollution problem their primary concern. It would be
difficult to see the rest of Texas and Louisiana legislating stricter
automotive controls for the benefit of the coastal areas, but such
action may be required. Coastal-zone planning by the states to pro-
tect their beach and marsh areas, active local concern with an effective voice of urban dwellers, and participation by the fishing industry and other affected groups are all elements of better environmental protection.

PETROLEUM IMPORTS

These tentative conclusions are based on the continuing high
price of oil and a modest increase of imports. Any departure from
this slow-growth future, or an inability to maintain domestic production, will alter the conclusions.

Modest growth and the completion of one or two Gulf Coast
ports will reinforce the South as the center of petroleum refining
and chemical activity. The South should gain in jobs and income.
The secondary- and tertiary-development benefits will offset the
environmental risks. The East Coast, however, will not generate
the job and income benefits in the same proportion under the slow-
growth future where Gulf Coast ports are in operation. Having made
a continued commitment in the South, the petroleum and chemical industries are not likely to redirect investment to the East Coast. The
East Coast investment may include ports and refineries sufficient
to serve petroleum markets, but much of the imports are likely to
be in the form of products and bulk delivery of chemicals; the processing will be done elsewhere.

The chemical industry will depend upon the petroleum industry
for raw materials and site plants near their access to supplies.
Emerging petroleum-industry decisions are likely to influence the
chemical industry, which will reinforce the commitment to the Gulf

Coast. Once these interindustry decision processes are set in motion, it will take more than the marginal cost of transport to reverse these decisions. Only rapidly increasing dependence on foreign supplies over a long period of time will require a reappraisal of industries' outlooks.

The other factor is that the status quo is relatively safe. If the East Coast states and regions hold the door open for development, then industry is in a position to reassess their future. As long as the door is closed, reassessment is not necessary. Given the much larger constraints of secure and continuous raw-material supplies, the problem of foreign dependence, and the inability to control prices, the siting problem is a dependent rather than independent variable. State environmental and development policy is only one of the factors in industry decisions.

From the perspective of states and regions, it is far more important to define how development occurs than to know what industry intentions are. Since the uncertain world cannot predetermine what will be offered, deliberate efforts to define state and regional goals become more important. Public debate, broad exposure of issues, and an active interest in government make this definition possible. Attention to how the process is conducted, to the players involved, and to the interests not represented is crucial. Explicit recognition that policymaking is conducted through organized interests in society helps to focus on the dilemma of the unorganized or unexpressed interests. Decisions being made at a given point in time rarely involve all groups and views that should be represented. It is only when these decisions run the gauntlet of public inspection and interest-group pressure that they take on the semblance of public policy.

NOTES

1. Peter Amory Bradford, Fragile Structures: A Story of Oil Refineries, National Security and the Coast of Maine (New York: Harper's Magazine Press, 1975).

2. Ibid., p. 121. Bradford includes an interesting story of how a 30,000 b/d refinery was built in Hawaii through Stewart Udall, who against President Johnson's wishes directed an aide to publish the refinery permit approval in the Federal Register while Johnson attended Nixon's inauguration.

3. Ibid., pp. 132-33. Bradford mentions the important exception of Gardiner C. Means, a Maine resident and author with A. A. Berle of The Modern Corporation and Private Property (New York: Commerce Clearing House, 1952). Means took an active role in planning. Among other things he developed environmental

regulations for the Machias Port Conservation and Planning Committee.

4.   David B. Truman, The Governmental Process (New York: Alfred A. Knopf, 1951), p. 439.

5.   Bradford, op. cit., pp. 263-64.   State standards have been stricter than federal law in the air-pollution laws and standards set by the California Air Resources Board.

SELECTED BIBLIOGRAPHY

AIR QUALITY

Environmental Protection Agency. "Air Quality Implementation Plans: Prevention of Significant Air Quality Deterioration." Federal Register 39, no. 235 (December 5, 1974).

_____. Background Information for Proposed New Source Performance Standards. 3 Vols. Research Triangle Park, N.C., June 1973.

_____. Compilation of Air Pollution Emission Factors. Research Triangle Park, N.C., 1972.

_____. Compilation of Air Pollution Emission Factors: Supplement No. 5. Research Triangle Park, N.C., December 1975.

Jones, Harold R. Pollution Control in the Petroleum Industry. Park Ridge, N.J.: Noyes Data Corporation, 1973.

National Environmental Research Center. Atmospheric Emissions from the Petroleum Refining Industry. Springfield, Va.: National Technical Information Service, August 1973.

Nutkowitz, Paul. Air Quality in the Tri-State Region. New York: Tri-State Regional Planning Commission, 1974.

ARTICLES

Aalund, Leo R. "Grass Roots Project Reflects New Era." Oil and Gas Journal 73, no. 4 (January 27, 1975).

Akins, J. E. "International Cooperative Efforts in Energy Supply." Annals of the American Academy of Social and Political Science 410 (November 1973): 75-85.

Berg, R. R.; R. C. Calhoun; and J. L. Whiting. "Prognosis for Expanded U.S. Production of Crude Oil." Science 184 (April 19, 1974): 330-36.

Butler, James N. "Pelagic Tar." Scientific American 232, no. 6
    (June 1975): 90-97.

Chandler, Geoffrey. "The Changing Shape of the Petroleum Industry."
    Petroleum Review, formerly Institute of Petroleum Review
    (June 1974).

Chenery, Hollis B. "Restructuring the World Economy." Foreign
    Affairs 53 (January 1975): 242-63.

Gemaassmer, A. M. "The Petrochemical Industry in the Federal
    Republic of Germany." Journal of the Institute of Petroleum
    (November 1970).

"The Hottest Items on the Shelf: LNG Carriers." Fortune 87 (April
    1973): 60-61.

Jacobson, Jay, and Gregory P. Salottolo. "Petrochemical Oxidents
    in the New York-New Jersey Region." Atmospheric Environ-
    ment 9, no. 3 (April 1975).

Jenkins, Gilbert. "The Spot Market for Tankers." Petroleum Re-
    view (January 1974).

Kraar, Louis. "OPEC Is Starting to Feel the Pressure." Fortune
    91 (May 1975): 186-91.

Kuhl, H. J. "Structure of Petroleum Refining in Western Germany."
    Journal of the Institute of Petroleum (November 1970).

Levy, Walter. "World Cooperation or International Chaos." For-
    eign Affairs 52, no. 4 (July 1974): 690-713.

Lincoln, G. A. "Energy Conservation." Science 180, no. 4082
    (April 13, 1973): 155-62.

Mattilla, John M. "A Metropolitan Income Determination Model and
    the Estimation of Metropolitan Income Multipliers." Journal
    of Regional Science 13, no. 1 (1973).

McDonald, John. "Oil and Environment: The View from Maine."
    Fortune (April 1971): 84-89.

Nelson, W. L. "Cost of Refineries." Oil and Gas Journal (July
    29, 1974).

"New Trend toward Construction in Producing Areas." Petroleum
    Economist (September 1974).

Robinson, B. W. "Planning for a Refining Project." Petroleum
    Review (March 1973).

Stewart, Matthew F., and James T. Jensen. "Chemical Refinery in
    Perspective." Refining Petroleum for Chemicals. Advances in
    Chemistry Series 97: A Symposium, September 10-12, 1969
    (Washington, D.C.: American Chemical Society, 1970), pp. 123-
    123-39.

Weille, Jan de, and Anandarup Ray. "The Optimum Port Capacity."
    Journal of Transport Economics and Public Policy (September
    1974).

Wennick, Captain. "Superports of Europe." Petroleum Review
    (January 1974).

Wett, Ted. "The Petrochemical Report." Oil and Gas Journal
    (1973-75).

CONGRESSIONAL REPORTS AND HEARINGS

U.S. Congress, House. Deepwater Ports. Report together with
    supplemental views from Committee on Public Works to ac-
    company H.R. 10701, November 28, 1973.

_____. H.R. 10701, An Act, ordered to be printed with amendments
    of the Senate, October 9, 1974.

_____. Committee on Merchant Marine and Fisheries. Offshore
    Ports and Terminals. 93d Cong., 1st sess., 1973, hearing
    on H.R. 5091 and H.R. 5898.

_____. Committee on Public Works. Deepwater Ports. Joint hear-
    ings before the Subcommittee on Water Resources and Sub-
    committee on Energy, 93d Cong., 1st sess., 1973, H.R. 10701.

_____. Committee on Science and Astronautics. Energy Facts.
    Prepared for Subcommittee on Energy by the Science Policy
    Research Division. 93d Cong., 1st sess., 1973.

U.S. Congress, Senate. Committee on Commerce. 1973 IMCO
    Conference on Marine Pollution from Ships. 93d Cong., 1st
    sess., 1973.

_____. Committee on Interior and Insular Affairs. Deepwater Port Policy Issues. A Staff Analysis prepared at the request of Henry M. Jackson, Chairman. 93d Cong., 2nd sess., 1974.

_____. Committee on Public Works. Deepwater Ports. Hearing before Subcommittee on Air and Water Pollution. 93d Cong., 1st sess., S. 180 and S. 836, February 26, 1973.

_____. Committee on Science and Astronautics. Report of the Task Force on Energy. Committee Print, 92nd Cong., 1972.

_____. Committees on Commerce, Interior and Insular Affairs and Public Works. Deepwater Port Act of 1973, 2 parts. Joint hearings before the Special Joint Subcommittee on Deepwater Port Legislation. 93d Cong., 1st sess., on S. 1751 and S. 2232, 1973.

_____. Deepwater Port Policy Issues. Hearing, 92nd Cong., 2nd sess., pursuant to S. Res. 45. National Fuels and Energy Policy Study, April 25, 1972.

_____. Fuel Shortages. Parts I and II. Hearing, 93d Cong., 1st sess., pursuant to S. Res. 45. National Fuels and Energy Policy Study, 1973.

_____. Oil and Gas Import Issues. Parts I-III. Hearings 92d Cong., 1972.

_____. Subcommittee on Environmental Pollution. Implementation of Transportation Controls. 3 vols. Hearing before 93d Cong., 2nd sess., Serial No. 93-H29, May 1974.

_____. Toward a Rational Policy of Oil and Gas Imports. Committee Print, 93d Cong., Serial 93-94, 1973.

_____. U.S. Energy Resources: A Review as of 1972. M. K. Hubbert.

DEEPWATER PORTS: REPORTS

Adler, Hans A. Economic Appraisal of Transport Projects: A Manual with Case Studies. Bloomington, Ind.: Indiana University Press, 1971.

Bradford, Peter Amory. Fragile Structures: A Story of Oil Refineries, National Security and the Coast of Maine. New York:
Harper's Magazine Press, 1975.

Bragaw, Louis K.; Henry S. Marcus; Gary C. Raffaele; and James
R. Townley. The Challenge of Deepwater Terminals.
Lexington, Mass.: D. C. Heath, 1975.

Burmah Oil. "Information and Regulations of Burmah Oil." Bahamas
Terminal at South Riding Point, Grand Bahama. Mimeographed.

De Frondeville, Betrand L. Foreign Deepwater Port Developments.
3 vols. Prepared for the Institute of Water Resources. Washington, D.C.: Corps of Engineers, 1971.

Economic Development Administration. "Deepwater Terminal,
Anasco, Puerto Rico." Mimeographed.

Gifford, Corydon Rouse. An Investigation: U.S. Import Dependence
for Mineral Resources: "Super" Bulk Carriers and Deepwater
Port Developments. Naval Post Graduate School. Springfield,
Va.: National Technical Information Service, 1973.

Heggie, I. G., and C. B. Edwards. "Port Investment Problems:
How to Decide Investment Priorities." Conference on Civil
Engineering Problems Overseas. Session V, paper no. 3
(1968).

H. J. Kaiser Company and Gulf South Research Institute. The Economic Impact of a Louisiana Offshore Oil Port. Baton Rouge,
La., 1973.

Kenyon, James. "Elements of Inter-port Competition in the United
States." Economic Geography 46 (January 1970).

Klausner, Robert F. "The Evaluation of Risk in Marine Capital Investment." The Engineering Economist 14, no. 4 (Summer
1969).

Little, Arthur D. Foreign Deepwater Port Developments. 3 vols.
Prepared for the Corps of Engineers. Springfield, Va.:
National Technical Information Service, 1971.

_____. Potential Onshore Effects of Deepwater Oil Terminal-Related
Industrial Development. 5 vols. Prepared for the Council on

Environmental Quality. Springfield, Va.: National Technical
Information Service, 1973.

LOOP, Inc. Application for License. 22 vols. Washington, D.C.:
U.S. Coast Guard, 1975.

Meyer, John R. Techniques of Transport Planning. Washington,
D.C.: Brookings, 1971.

M.I.T. A Preliminary Assessment of the Environmental Vulnerability of Machias Bay, Maine. Springfield, Va.: National
Technical Information Service, 1973.

Plumlee, Carl H. "Optimum Size Seaport." Journal of the Waterways and Harbor Division (August 1966).

Robert R. Nathan Associates. U.S. Deepwater Port Study. 5 vols.
Prepared for U.S. Department of the Army, Corps of En-
gineers, Institute for Water Resources. Springfield, Va.:
National Technical Information Service, 1972.

SEADOCK, Inc. Application for License. 5 vols. Washington,
D.C.: U.S. Coast Guard, 1975.

Shoup, Donald S. Ports and Economic Development. Washington,
D.C.: Brookings, 1967.

SOROS Associates. Offshore Terminal System Concepts. New
York, 1972.

State University of New York at Stony Brook. Possible Effects of
Construction and Operation of a Supertanker Terminal on the
Marine Environment in the New York Bight. Springfield, Va.:
National Technical Information Service, 1973.

Taaffee, Edward, and Howard L. Gauthier. Geography of Transportation. Englewood Cliffs, N.J.: Prentice-Hall, 1973.

Texas A & M University. Environmental Aspects of a Supertanker
Port on the Texas Gulf Coast. Springfield, Va.: National
Technical Information Service, 1973.

Transportation Concepts and Techniques. "Proposal for Development of Crude Oil Transfer Terminal." Little Cayman Island,
British West Indies. Mimeographed.

U.S. Department of Commerce. The Economics of Deepwater
    Terminals. Washington, D.C.: U.S. Government Printing
    Office, 1972.

U.S. Department of the Interior. Draft Environmental Impact
    Statement: Deepwater Ports. Washington, D.C., June 1973.

University of Delaware. Environmental Vulnerability of the Delaware
    Bay Area to Supertanker Accommodation. 4 vols. Springfield,
    Va.: National Technical Information Service, 1973.

Van Houton Associates, Inc. Economic and Engineering Analysis
    for Delivery of Refined Products. For U.S. Army Corps of
    Engineers, Philadelphia district, March 1973.

ENERGY

Fisher, J. C. Energy Crisis in Perspective. New York: John
    Wiley, 1974.

Ford Foundation. A Time to Choose. Cambridge, Mass.: Ballinger,
    1974.

Freeman, S. David. Energy: The New Era. New York: Random
    House, Vintage Books, 1974.

Hobson, G. D., and W. Pohl, eds. Modern Petroleum Technology.
    New York: John Wiley, 1973.

Meadows, Donella H.; Dennis L. Meadows; Jorgen Randers; and
    William W. Behrens, III. The Limits to Growth. Washing-
    ton, D.C.: Potomac Associates, 1972.

Petroleum Publishing Company. International Petroleum Encyclo-
    pedia. Tulsa, Okla., 1973.

Schurr, Sam H., ed. Energy, Economic Growth and the Environ-
    ment: Resources for the Future. Baltimore: Johns Hopkins
    Press, 1972.

_____, and B. Hetchert. Energy in the American Economy 1850-
    1975. Baltimore: Johns Hopkins Press, 1960.

University of Oklahoma. Energy Under the Oceans. Norman,
    Okla.: University of Oklahoma Press, 1973.

Waddams, A. Lawrence. Chemicals from Petroleum. 3rd ed.
    New York: John Wiley, 1973.

ENERGY: REPORTS

American Petroleum Institute. Annual Statistical Review: U.S.
    Petroleum Statistics 1956-1972. Washington, D.C., April
    1973.

Anderson, Kent P. Toward Econometric Estimation of Industrial
    Energy Demand: An Experimental Application to Primary
    Metals Industry. Santa Monica, Calif.: Rand Corporation,
    December 1971.

Cabinet Task Force on Oil Import Control. The Oil Import Question.
    Washington, D.C.: U.S. Government Printing Office, 1970.

The Conference Board. Energy and Public Policy--1972. John J.
    Murphy, ed. New York, 1972.

Data Resources, Inc. A Study of the Quarterly Demand for Gasoline
    and Impacts of Alternative Gasoline Taxes. Lexington, Mass.,
    December 1973.

Energy Policy Project of the Ford Foundation. Exploring Energy
    Choices: A Preliminary Report. Washington, D.C.: Ford
    Foundation, 1974.

Federal Energy Administration. Project Independence. Washington,
    D.C.: U.S. Government Printing Office, November 1974.

Hirst, Eric. Direct and Indirect Energy Requirements for Automo-
    biles. Oak Ridge, Tenn.: Oak Ridge National Laboratory,
    April 1973.

Mooz, W. E., and C. C. Mow. California's Electricity Quandary:
    Estimating Future Demand. Santa Monica, Calif.: Rand
    Corporation, 1972.

National Petroleum Council. Factors Affecting U.S. Petroleum Re-
    fining: A Summary. H.A. True, Chairman. Washington,
    D.C., 1973.

_____. U.S. Energy Outlook. Washington, D.C., December 1972.

Stanford Research Institute. Patterns of Energy Consumption in the
    United States. Prepared for the Office of Science and Technol-
    ogy. Washington, D.C.: U.S. Government Printing Office,
    1972.

Tichansky, Dennis P. Methods for Estimating the Volume and Energy
    Demand of Freight Transportation. Santa Monica, Calif.: Rand
    Corporation, December 1972.

U.S. Atomic Energy Commission. The Nation's Energy Future.
    Dr. Dixy Lee Ray, Chairman. Washington, D.C.: U.S. Gov-
    ernment Printing Office, December 1973.

U.S. Department of the Interior. Petroleum Refineries in the United
    States. Washington, D.C.: Bureau of Mines, January 1972.

U.S. Department of Transportation. Energy Statistics. Prepared
    by the Office of the Secretary. Springfield, Va.: National
    Technical Information Service, September 1973.

                            GAME THEORY

Davis, Morton D. Game Theory: A Non-Technical Introduction.
    New York: Basic Books, 1970.

McDonald, John. The Game of Business. Garden City, N.Y.:
    Doubleday, 1975.

Rapoport, Anatol. N-Person Game Theory: Concepts and Applica-
    tions. Ann Arbor, Mich.: University of Michigan Press, 1970.

Riker, William H. The Theory of Political Coalitions. New Haven:
    Yale University Press, 1962.

Schelling, Thomas C. The Strategy of Conflict. Cambridge, Mass.:
    Harvard University Press, 1960.

Shubik, Martin. Game Theory and Related Approaches to Human
    Behavior. New York: John Wiley, 1964.

_____. Strategy and Market Structure. New York: John Wiley,
    1959.

Von Neumann, John, and Oskar Morgenstern. The Theory of Games
2nd ed. Princeton, N.J.: Princeton University Press, 1947.

Williams, John Davis. The Compleat Strategyst. Rev. ed. New
York: McGraw-Hill, 1966.

PETROLEUM ECONOMICS

Adelman, M. A. The World Petroleum Market. Baltimore: Johns
Hopkins Press, 1972.

Baldwin, Robert. Nontariff Distortions of International Trade.
Washington, D.C.: Brookings, 1970.

Foster Associates, Inc. Energy Prices: 1960-1973. Cambridge,
Mass.: Ballinger, 1974.

Frankel, Paul H. Essentials of Petroleum. London: Chapman and
Hall, 1969.

Hartshorne, J. E. Politics and World Oil Economics. London:
Faber and Faber, 1967.

Issawi, Charles. The Economics of Middle Eastern Oil. New York:
Praeger, 1973.

Jacoby, Neil. Multi-National Oil. New York: Macmillan, 1974.

National Petroleum News. Factbook. New York: McGraw-Hill,

Petroleum Press Service. The Petroleum Economist. London:
Petroleum Press Foundation (monthly), 1974.

Platt's Oilgram Price Service. Platt's Oilgram. New York:
McGraw-Hill, daily.

_____. Platt's Oilgram, 50th ed. New York: McGraw-Hill, 1974.

Seifert, William W.; Mohammed A. Bakr; and M. Ali Kettani.
Energy and Development: A Case Study. Cambridge, Mass.:
M.I.T. Press, 1973.

United Nations. The Petrochemical Industry. New York, 1973.

Zannetos, Zenon S. The Theory of Oil Tankship Rates. Cambridge, Mass.: M.I.T. Press, 1966.

POLITICS AND POLICY

Boren, James H. When in Doubt, Mumble: A Bureaucrat's Handbook. New York: Van Nostrand Reinhold, 1974.

Burkhead, Jesse, and Jerry Miner. Public Expenditure. Chicago: Aldine-Atherton, 1971.

Dahl, Robert, and C. E. Lindblom. Politics, Economics and Welfare. New York: Harper and Row, 1953.

Dickson, Paul. Think Tanks. New York: Atheneum, 1971.

Downs, Anthony. Inside Bureaucracy. Boston: Little, Brown, 1967.

Lindblom, C.E. The Intelligence of Democracy. New York: Free Press, 1967.

_____. The Policy Making Process. Englewood Cliffs, N.J.: Prentice-Hall, 1968.

_____, and D. Braybrooke. A Strategy of Decision. New York: Free Press, 1963.

March, J. G., and H. A. Simon. Organizations. New York: John Wiley, 1958.

McConnell, Grant. Private Power and American Democracy. New York: Alfred A. Knopf, 1966.

Truman, David B. The Governmental Process. New York: Alfred A. Knopf, 1951.

Wildavsky, Aaron. "The Political Economy of Efficiency: Cost Benefit Analysis, Systems Analysis and Program Budgeting." Public Administration Review 26 (December 1966).

_____. The Politics of the Budgetary Process. Boston: Little, Brown, 1964.

Wilensky, Harold L. Organizational Intelligence. New York: Basic Books, 1967.

REGIONAL ECONOMICS

Friedman, John, and William Alonso. Regional Development and
     Planning. Cambridge, Mass.: M.I.T. Press, 1964.

Greenhut, Melvin. Microeconomics and the Space Economy: The
     Effectiveness of an Oligopolistic Market. Chicago: Scott,
     Foresman, 1963.

_____. A Theory of the Firm in Economic Space. New York:
     McGraw-Hill, 1948.

Highway Research Board. Highway Capacity Manual. Washington,
     D.C., 1965.

Hoover, Edgar M. The Location of Economic Activity. New York:
     Appleton-Century-Crofts, 1970.

Isard, Walter. Methods of Regional Analysis: An Introduction to
     Regional Science. Cambridge, Mass.: M.I.T. Press, 1960.

_____; Charles L. Choquill; John Kissin; Richard H. Seyforth; and
     Richard Tatlock. Ecologic-Economic Analysis for Regional
     Development. New York: Free Press, 1972.

_____, and Eugene W. Schooler. Location Factors in the Petro-
     chemical Industry. Washington, D.C.: Office of Technical
     Services, U.S. Department of Commerce, 1955.

_____; Eugene W. Schooler; and Thomas Victorisz. Industrial
     Complex Analysis and Regional Development with Particular
     Reference to Puerto Rico. New York: John Wiley, 1959.

Needleman, L., ed. Regional Analysis: A Reader. Baltimore:
     Penguin Books, 1968.

Nourse, Hugh. Regional Economics. New York: McGraw-Hill,
     1968.

Ogburn, William F. Culture and Social Change. Otis Dudley
     Duncan, ed. Chicago: University of Chicago Press, 1964.

Richardson, Harry W., ed. Regional Economics: A Reader.
     London: Macmillan, St. Martin's Press, 1970.

Thompson, Wilbur. A Preface to Urban Economics. Baltimore:
    Johns Hopkins Press, 1965.

                              TANKSHIPS

The British Petroleum Company. BP Statistical Review of the
    World Oil Industry--1972. London: Brittanic House, Moor
    Lane.

Esso International. Investigation of High Depth Segregated Ballast
    Tankers by T. A. Goddard, Project Engineer for Maritime
    Administration, Department of Commerce. Linden, N.J.,
    July 1971.

Fearnley and Egers Chartering Co. Ltd. Review 1975. Oslo,
    Norway, January 1976.

H. Clarkson and Co. Ltd. The Tanker Register. London, 1971.

H. P. Dewry Ltd. Repairing and Drydocking Large Carriers, no.
    23. London, 1974.

_____. Seasonal Fluctuations in Crude Products and Tanker De-
    mand, no. 30. London, March 1975.

_____. The Trading Outlook for Very Large Tankers, no. 32.
    London, July 1975.

_____. World Shipbuilding Output and Capacity, no. 33. London,
    1975.

John I. Jacobs and Co. Ltd. World Tanker Fleet Review. London,
    June 1975.

Lambert Brothers Shipping Ltd. A Review of Developments in
    World Trade and Their Effect on the Shipping Market.
    London, September 1974.

Mostert, Noel. Supertanker. New York: Alfred A. Knopf, 1974.

Office of Technology Assessment. Oil Transportation by Tankers:
    An Analysis of Marine Pollution Safety Measures. Springfield,
    Va.: National Technical Information Service, July 1975.

Organisation for Economic Co-operation and Development. Maritime Transport 1973. Paris, 1974.

Sun Oil Company. Analysis of World Tank Ship Fleet. St. Davids, Pa., October 1973.

_____. Corporate Development Group. Analysis of World Tank Ship Fleet: 1970. Philadelphia, August 1971.

U.S. Coast Guard. "New York Vessel Traffic System." Draft Environmental Impact Statement. New York, 1974.

U.S. Department of Commerce. Essential United States Foreign Trade Routes. Washington, D.C.: U.S. Government Printing Office, December 1969.

_____. Maritime Administration. "Tanker Construction Program." Draft Environmental Impact Statement I. Washington, D.C., n.d.

U.S. Department of Transportation. "Certain Tank Vessels: Proposed Rules." Federal Register 41, no. 74 (April 15, 1976).

_____. "Deepwater Ports." Federal Register 40, no. 217 (November 10, 1975).

THEORY AND ECONOMETRICS

Baumol, William J. Economic Theory and Operations Analysis. 2nd ed. Englewood Cliffs, N.J.: Prentice-Hall, 1965.

Chase Econometrics Association, Inc., et al. The Economic Impact of Pollution Control: A Summary of Recent Studies. Prepared for the Council of Environmental Quality, Department of Commerce, and Environmental Protection Agency. Washington, D.C.: U.S. Government Printing Office, March 1972.

Data Resources, Inc. A Study of the Quarterly Demand for Gasoline and Impacts of Alternative Gasoline Taxes. Lexington, Mass.: Data Resources, Inc., December 1973.

Ferguson, C. E. Microeconomic Theory. Rev. ed. Homewood, Ill.: Richard D. Irwin, 1969.

Houthakker, H. S., and Lester D. Taylor. Consumer Demand in the United States: 1929-1970. Cambridge, Mass.: Harvard University Press, 1966.

Kane, Edward J. Economic Statistics and Econometrics. New York: Harper and Row, 1968.

Klein, Lawrence R. An Introduction to Econometrics. Englewood Cliffs, N.J.: Prentice-Hall, 1962.

Stigler, George. The Theory of Price. New York: Macmillan, 1952.

Wold, Herman, and Lars Jureen. Demand Analysis. New York: John Wiley, 1953.

WATER QUALITY AND RISK ANALYSIS

Ackerman, Bruce, and James Sawyer. "The Uncertain Search for Environmental Policy: Scientific Factfinding and Rational Decisionmaking Along the Delaware River." Environmental Law Review--1973. New York: Clark Boardman, 1973.

Allan, D. S.; A. A. Brown; and P. Athens. "Risks Associated with an LNG Shipping Operation." Presented at the Fourth International Symposium on Transport of Hazardous Cargoes by Sea and Inland Waterways. New Orleans, April 1975. Mimeographed.

American Petroleum Institute; Environmental Protection Agency; and the U.S. Coast Guard. Prevention and Control of Oil Spills. Proceedings of Joint Conference. Washington, D.C.: American Petroleum Institute, March 1973.

Boesch, Donald G.; Carl Hershner; and Jerome H. Milgram. Oil Spills in the Marine Environment. Cambridge, Mass.: Ballinger, 1974.

Bosselman, Fred, and David Callies. The Quiet Revolution in Land Use Control. Washington, D.C.: U.S. Government Printing Office, 1972.

Council of Environmental Quality. "National Pollution Contingency Plan." Federal Register. Washington, D.C., February 10, 1975.

Davis, George H., and Leonard A. Wood. Water Demands for Expanding Energy Development. Geological Survey Circular 703. Reston, Va.: U.S. Geological Survey, 1974.

Exxon. Reducing Tanker Accidents. New York: Public Affairs Department, September 1973.

_____. "Safer Tankers and Cleaner Seas." New York: Public Affairs Department, December 1972.

Federal Water Pollution Control Administration. U.S. Department of the Interior. Delaware Estuary Comprehensive Study. 1966.

Inter-Governmental Maritime Consultative Organization. Final Act of the International Conference on Marine Pollution, 1973. London, November 1973. Mimeographed.

J. J. Henry Company. An Analysis of Oil Outflows Due to Tanker Accidents, 1971-1972. Prepared for the U.S. Coast Guard. Springfield, Va.: National Technical Information Service, 1973.

Keith, V. F., and J. D. Porricelli. "An Analysis of Oil Outflows Due to Tanker Accidents." Prevention and Control of Oil Spills. Proceedings of a joint conference of the American Petroleum Institute, Environmental Protection Agency, and U.S. Coast Guard. Washington, D.C., March 1973.

Little, Arthur D. Analysis of Probability of Collisions, Rammings and Groundings of the LNG Barge Massachusetts. Report to Brooklyn Union Gas Company, Consolidated Edison Company of New York, and Distrigas Corporation. Cambridge, Mass., October 1974.

M.I.T. Offshore Oil Task Group. The Georges Bank Petroleum Study. Vol. 2. Cambridge, Mass.: M.I.T. Seagrant Project, February 1973.

National Academy of Sciences. Ocean Affairs Board. Petroleum in the Marine Environment. Washington, D.C.: National Academy of Sciences, 1975.

_____. Committee on Water Quality Criteria. Water Quality Criteria 1972. Washington, D.C.: U.S. Government Printing Office, 1972.

National Science Foundation. Pollutant Transfer to the Marine En-
    vironment. International Decade of Ocean Exploration Pollu-
    tant Transfer Workshop, January 11-12, 1974. Kingston,
    R.I., 1974.

Nelson-Smith, A. Oil Pollution and the Marine Ecology. New York:
    Plenum Press, 1973.

Page, R. C., and Ward A. Gardiner. Petroleum Tankship Safety.
    London: The Maritime Press Ltd., 1971.

Pearson, Charles S. International Marine Environmental Policy:
    The Economic Dimension. Baltimore: The Johns Hopkins
    Press, 1975.

Rasmussen, Norman C. Draft Reactor Safety Study: An Assess-
    ment of Accident Risks in U.S. Commercial Nuclear Power
    Plants. Washington, D.C.: U.S. Atomic Energy Commission,
    August 1974.

ABOUT THE AUTHOR

TOBEY L. WINTERS has worked on economic and environmental aspects of transportation at Tri-State Regional Planning Commission in New York City. He has a special interest in the economic, marketing, and social issues in public transportation, including such topics as the interface of transportation, air quality, and fuel conservation. Prior to joining the Tri-State staff, Mr. Winters worked for the engineering consulting firm of Wilbur Smith and Associates.

The author received an A.B. in Political Science and a Ph.D. in Social Science from Syracuse University. The latter was in an interdisciplinary program of economics, public administration, and metropolitan studies.

Mr. Winters served two years in the Peace Corps as a business advisor to agricultural cooperative societies in Kenya.

ALTERNATIVE ENERGY STRATEGIES: Constraints and Opportunities
John Hagel, III

ARAB OIL: Impact on Arab Countries and Global Implications
edited by Naiem A. Sherbiny
Mark A. Tessler

MANAGEMENT OF TRANSPORTATION CARRIERS
Grant M. Davis
Martin T. Farris
Jack J. Holder, Jr.

PRESERVATION VERSUS DEVELOPMENT:
An Economic Analysis of San Francisco Bay Wetlands
Ralph Andrew Luken

THE PRICING OF CRUDE OIL: Economic and Strategic Guidelines for an International Energy Policy (expanded and updated edition)
Taki Rifaï